Employment revival in Europe

Employment revival in Europe

Labour market success in Austria, Denmark, Ireland and the Netherlands

Peter Auer

 INTERNATIONAL LABOUR OFFICE • GENEVA

Auer, P.
Employment revival in Europe: Labour market success in Austria, Denmark, Ireland and the Netherlands
Geneva, International Labour Office, 2000
Employment, unemployment, promotion of employment, labour market, employment policy, labour policy, Austria, Denmark, Ireland, Netherlands. 13.01.3

ISBN 92-2-110841-4

ILO Cataloguing-in-Publication Data

ILO publications can be obtained through major booksellers or ILO local offices in many countries, or direct from ILO Publications, International Labour Office, CH-1211 Geneva 22, Switzerland. Catalogues or lists of new publications are available free of charge from the above address.

FOREWORD

This comparative study is part of the International Labour Office's follow-up activities to Commitment Three of the Declaration and Programme of Action of the World Summit for Social Development, held in Copenhagen in 1995. Commitment Three reiterates the importance of full, productive and freely chosen employment as a basic condition for social progress. The ILO was chosen from the United Nations organizations to monitor the progress made by countries in fulfilling this Commitment. It is well placed to play an active role in this area, as Commitment Three conforms largely to an earlier ILO instrument adopted in 1964 (the Employment Policy Convention, No. 122).

As well as drafting country employment policy reviews (CEPRs) in the developing and transition countries, the ILO decided to study the progress of employment policies in certain countries of the Organisation for Economic Co-operation and Development (OECD). Among those experiencing improvements in their labour markets, four smaller European countries (Austria, Denmark, Ireland and the Netherlands) were finally chosen. Unlike some larger European countries, these four have been experiencing a remarkable labour market recovery or have maintained low unemployment over the long term.

The study shows that the relative labour market success of the four countries is due in particular to three policy areas: social dialogue, macroeconomic policy and labour market policy. Social dialogue created a climate of confidence among the principal social actors; this is particularly visible in the countries that suffered a major economic and labour market crisis before their present recovery. It is only after this crisis that social concertation was put in place or reinvigorated, and economic recovery started that finally resulted in labour market recovery.

The new climate of confidence led to wage moderation and to reforms in social protection systems. Wage moderation was part and parcel of a stabilization-oriented macroeconomic policy which led to low inflation and low interest rates. Labour market policy (and social protection in general) created the necessary flexibility for labour market adjustment.

While the four countries differ in many respects and have by no means achieved "the best of all worlds", they have made progress towards the goal of full employment. Although much still remains to be done, these countries have shown that employment success is also feasible in Europe's Welfare States that maintain a balance between efficiency and equity issues.

Werner Sengenberger,
Director,
Employment Strategy Department,
International Labour Office,
Geneva

CONTENTS

Contents

List of tables

Contents

List of figures

PREFACE AND ACKNOWLEDGEMENTS

This book presents the results of ILO country employment policy reviews (CEPRs) in four European countries (Austria, Denmark, Ireland and the Netherlands). The four country studies have been reviewed and commented on by the social partners and ministries of labour in the countries concerned. These countries were selected with the approval of the Governing Body of the ILO, mainly because they have recently improved their labour market situation considerably, or have a good labour market record over the long term. The factors explaining their relative success merit attention and might indicate new solutions to a problem which has afflicted Europe for the last two decades.

The main aim of the study is thus to analyse this success and the factors which can explain it. As success is relative, both in relation to certain benchmarks and between countries, and might have trade-offs in terms of economic or social costs, the analysis of success is as important as its explanation. The analysis of the progress made towards the goal of full employment and decent work, and the explanation of the factors underlying success or failure, are at the heart of the present study.

Following from the aims outlined above, the present study contains four main parts: an introduction; an analysis of labour market progress and of the remaining problems in the four countries; a discussion of the reasons for labour market success; and a conclusion with policy recommendations.

This book is based mainly on nine reports prepared for the comparative European CEPRs. Although they are not always explicitly cited, these reports constitute the main theoretical backbone of this book, which could not have been drafted without them. The nine reports are as follows:

1. Austria, by Dr. Karl Pichelmann and Helmut Hofer, Institute for Advanced Studies (IHS), Vienna. (Since 1999, Dr. Pichelmann has been adviser for employment questions at DG II of the European Commission.)
2. Denmark, by Professor Per K. Madsen, University of Copenhagen.

3. Ireland, by Dr. Philip O'Connell, Economic and Social Research Institute, Dublin.
4. The Netherlands, by Professor Joop Hartog, University of Amsterdam.
5. Industrial relations, by Professor Jelle Visser, Max Planck Institute for Social Research, Cologne, and University of Amsterdam.
6. Macroeconomic policy, by Professor Ronald Schettkat, University of Utrecht.
7. Equal opportunity and employment policy, by Professor Jill Rubery, University of Manchester.
8. Working-time policies, by Professor Gerhard Bosch, Institute for Work and Technology, Gelsenkirchen.

Reports 1–4 are country reports, and reports 5–8 are thematic reports. Nos 5, 6, 7 and 8 will be published as a follow-up to the present volume.

The study also draws on a paper prepared by Sylvia Walter, "Taxation and the labour market", and on an important statistical overview of the four countries, which was prepared by Anita Guelfi (now at the Institute for Advanced Studies in Vienna). Arne Klau and the KILM (Key Indicators of the Labour Market) team of ILO/POLEMP also helped with statistics.

The study was also amply discussed in an ILO symposium held on the four successful countries (The Social Dialogue and Employment Success, an ILO symposium, Geneva, 2–3 March 1999) and I thank all the delegates for their active participation. When possible, their enriching remarks have been incorporated into the present volume.

In addition, the so-called "gatekeepers" in the ministries of labour of the four countries were of tremendous help in providing material, assistance, comments and support during the course of the study. These were, respectively, for Denmark, Mrs. Lone Adler, for Austria, Dr. Stefan Potmesil, for Ireland, Mr. Frank Doheny and for the Netherlands, Dr. Arthur van de Meerendonk.

I am also indebted for their comments to the members of the ILO advisory group, which was set up for the project. Members of this group were: Anne Trebilcock, Michael Cichon, Muneto Ozaki, Michael Henriques, Björn Grunewald, Heribert Scharrenbroich, Kim Eling, Riswanul Islam (represented by Steve Miller and Eric de Vries) and Bob Kyloh.

My thanks extend also to Werner Sengenberger, Gek-Boo Ng, Sandrine Cazes-Chaigne, Rolph van der Hoeven, Muhamed Muqtada, Niall O'Higgins, Zafar Shaheed and Hedva Sarfati who commented on the paper at different stages of its development.

Finally, I am also much indebted to Ghazwa Yousif (helped at times by Margaret Roberts, Anne Drougard and Lynda Pond) for typing and formatting the text. Editing was carried out by Andrew Watts and Susan Dunsmore, and the index was compiled by John Dawson. Despite this help, the sole responsibility for any mistakes remains with the author.

INTRODUCTION

1

The argument I advance is conditional. It applies primarily to the small corporatist states in Europe that, because of their open economies, have been vulnerable to shifts in the world economy during the twentieth century. Political stability and economic flexibility, I argue, are not contradictory but mutually contingent.

(Peter J. Katzenstein, *Small States in world markets*, 1985)

EUROPE'S REVIVAL

In the last 20 years the conventional wisdom has been that the European economy and labour market are "sclerotic", in stark contrast to the dynamic American labour market. The United States has experienced much higher growth rates of employment and markedly lower unemployment than Europe. Despite gross domestic product (GDP) growth rates which were comparable with the United States over the long term and at times even higher, economic growth contributed only very marginally to an expansion of employment. Unemployment also continued to grow in the European Union (EU), reaching around 11 per cent of the labour force in the middle of the nineties, and has only very recently started to fall below the 10 per cent threshold.

The reasons for American success were widely seen in its free market approach, low wage levels and high income differentiation. The prescription of leading economists for Europe was to use the same ingredients as those which were believed to be at the core of American success. Deregulation and privatization were to lead to a retreat of governments and the social partners – employers' and workers' organizations – from intervention in the markets. An entrepreneurial spirit, released from the strait-jacket of rules and regulations, and a wage policy left to the needs of the market would finally result in an improvement of the economy and the labour market and (re-) establish the positive dynamics of market forces everywhere.

Core elements of the European model, such as corporatist and often centralized collective bargaining leading to high and downwardly rigid wages, ever-expanding social and employment protection, and the strong role of the State in the socio-economy, were seen as the culprits in Europe's labour market problems. Unemployment was declared to be structural and voluntary, in the sense that rational actors in the labour markets would not take up work if there were alternatives of "making unemployment pay" in the form of over-generous benefits. In addition, high levels of public involvement and employment were denounced as displacing private initiatives, for example, in the services sector. Clearly, in such an approach there was no place for government to regulate the economy using monetary or fiscal policy. Aggregate demand was seen as the outcome of the interplay of market forces and if supply was flexible enough "it would create its own demand", as J.B. Say had postulated back in the nineteenth century. And according to the concept of the natural rate of unemployment (Friedmann, 1968), government intervention would only result in higher inflation. In a nutshell, the visible hand of government and the social partners should give way to the invisible hand of market forces.

While there was opposition in many European countries to the adoption of these supply-side policies, observers agree that during the last decade supply-side considerations have dominated the debate and have also been driving policy in Europe. A reminder of the major recent policy debates in Europe shows this quite strikingly. At the forefront of the debate and policy-making were supply-side reforms, deregulation, privatization and the curbing of public sector jobs rather than fiscal expansion, regulation, the extension of public employment and nationalization, and the expansion of the social security network. Countries such as France, which in the early 1980s put the policies of the "old" demand-side agenda into practice for a brief period, followed many of the prescriptions of the "new" supply-side agenda after 1982.

Today a number of smaller European countries have seen such a major fall in unemployment that one can speak of labour market recovery and relative success at last. Consequently, one of the questions of the present study is whether the application of the above policies has contributed to the success of the four countries under review. To be frank from the outset, we do not believe that recent labour market success can be categorically explained by the retreat of government and the social partners, by deregulation, privatization, reduced public sector jobs or lean organization. Although such policies have made a contribution to labour market success, the main explanation lies elsewhere: it is not the countries that have reduced social spending most, have curbed government intervention drastically or minimized social partnership that are the leading successes today. It is rather those which have retained, while adapting, their institutions, which now see their economic success spilling over into the labour market. It is therefore not the flexibility of the market, but the existence and adaptability of institutions and regulations which explain success in the cases reviewed. Contrary to widespread assumptions, these institutions were not in fact too rigid to survive in an environment demanding greater adaptability. The special European way of dealing with change, filtering it through established labour market institutions, leads to positive results. In other words, in Europe the "baby was not thrown out with the bathwater". The baby (institutions) was kept and the water (inefficiencies in the institutions) was at least partially thrown out. This accounts for a large part of European success.

SIMILARITIES AND DIFFERENCES

While one has to acknowledge that the countries of the EU have some important similarities (especially if one compares Europe to the United States or Japan) and have undergone a process of convergence, there is no unique "European model". The EU is in fact composed of 15 separate States, each with its own different national labour market institutions. Some of these countries exhibit greater institutional similarity with each other than with the rest, and although changes go in similar directions, there is an important element of national "path dependency". Institutions were carved out over many years and are the product of specific cultures, traditions and alliances, which serve to direct change processes.

This emerges from our study of four seemingly similar countries: they are all small open economies and members of the EU. Consequently, they have all oriented their macroeconomic policies towards meeting the Maastricht convergence criteria. Even though Denmark is not one of the first 11 countries participating in the Economic and Monetary Union (EMU), its monetary policy has already been aligned with that of the EMU members. All four countries have institutions of social partnership and an extensive net of social protection, and maintain a social dialogue between employers, unions and the government. All of them have signed the Copenhagen Declaration and its Programme of Action, and the earlier ILO Employment Policy Convention, 1964 (No. 122). Most importantly, they all place employment high on the agenda in accordance with the EU's Amsterdam Treaty and the conclusions of the Luxembourg Extraordinary Job Summit. Yet despite these similarities, important differences still remain. These will be pointed out in the following analysis. Therefore, the assumed homogeneity of the "European model", while it makes some sense if the EU is compared to other global players, gives way to considerable heterogeneity once the 15 countries are compared among themselves.

RELATIVE LABOUR MARKET SUCCESS

When can we speak of labour market success? Success is relative and multidimensional. Because of heterogeneity in countries' economies and institutions, there are also several ways to success. It can be measured over time, across countries and in relation to a target to be reached. Is a country more successful today than yesterday? Is it more successful than other countries? Is it more successful on the path to full employment? These are the three questions we must answer before addressing further issues. Such issues include: Why is a country successful? How did it overcome constraints? Does success in one area lead to problems in other areas (trade-offs)? And is success only short-lived or is it sustainable? The latter question implies that both starting levels, present levels and trends have to be looked at, as trends might develop from very different starting-points.

The target variable is clear: only when full employment is realized over a longer period of time can we speak of real labour market success. However, there are intermediary goals on the way to full employment and these goals are relative. Even so, we need a definition of full employment before we can measure countries according to this benchmark. The ILO definition of full employment is extensive, as it requires not only full employment but productive and freely chosen full employment. "Productive" refers either to regular private or public employment or to employment in labour market activities other than pure "make work" schemes. "Freely chosen" refers to a choice of employment with decent working conditions; it excludes all forced and compulsory work. According to Convention No. 122 and Commitment Three of the Copenhagen Declaration, full employment also means non-discriminatory employment: no discrimination should be allowed by the ratifying countries on the grounds of sex, age, religion or race (see annexes IV and V for the texts of these instruments).

Chapter 2 of the present report is devoted to a comparative analysis of the labour markets of the four countries. Chapter 3 will then discuss some of the reasons for the relative success of the four countries. Chapters 4 and 5 contain conclusions and policy recommendations.

EMPLOYMENT, UNEMPLOYMENT, INACTIVITY: A COMPARATIVE ASSESSMENT OF THE LABOUR MARKET

2

In terms of employment statistics, the whole population of working age is either employed, unemployed or inactive. In addition to the levels of activity and inactivity, the structure of employment, unemployment and inactivity is important. For an assessment of labour market success, the breakdown of employment into full-time, part-time, permanent and fixed-term work is pertinent. The same is true for the breakdown of the unemployed into short-term and long-term, as well as into entry and exit unemployed. The inactives are divided into those in education, those in early retirement or on invalidity pension, and those excluded from the labour market. All these benchmarks also have a gender and age dimension.

Table 2.1 gives an overview of the three basic labour market categories and their development between two points in time (1985–97). It shows the differences in the employment, unemployment and inactivity rates. All these rates are measured against the total population of working age. Unemployment rates are therefore lower than those usually reported, which are related merely to the labour force (e.g. the unemployed and the employed). Measuring the unemployed as in table 2.1 allows us to statistically represent 100 per cent of the working-age population. (Standardized labour force unemployment rates are presented under "Unemployment", pages 20 to 27, below.)

It appears that while the rank order between countries in gross employment rates (i.e. not adjusted for working time) did not change between 1985 and 1997 (in descending order, Denmark, Austria, the Netherlands, Ireland), Ireland and in particular the Netherlands have caught up. For example, the difference between the Netherlands and Austria declined from almost 10 percentage points in 1985 to a mere 2-point difference in 1997. Ireland still had employment rates below the EU average in 1997, but with a clear upward trend. Rank orders for inactivity are reversed (i.e. Denmark the lowest and Ireland the highest). Decline in inactivity is strongest in the Netherlands; Denmark actually experienced a slight increase in the inactivity rate, due probably to higher participation in full-time education. Austria leads

5

Table 2.1. Employment, unemployment and inactivity rates, 1985 and 1997 (as percentage of total population aged 15–64)

Country	Employment			Unemployment			Inactivity		
	1985	1997	Change	1985	1997	Change	1985	1997	Change
	Men and women								
Austria	67.3	69.9	+2.6	2.4	3.1	+0.7	30.3	27.0	−3.3
Denmark	77.4	77.5	0.1	5.8	4.9	−0.9	16.8	17.6	+0.8
Ireland	51.4	57.8	+6.4	10.5	6.5	−4.0	38.1	35.7	−2.4
Netherlands	57.7	66.7	+9.0	4.8	3.7	−0.9	37.5	29.6	−7.9
EU 15	59.8	60.5	+0.7	6.6	7.3	+0.7	33.6	32.2	−1.4
	Men								
Austria	83.1	80.4	−2.7	3.0	2.9	−0.1	13.9	16.7	+2.8
Denmark	85.4	83.9	−1.5	5.1	4.0	−0.9	9.5	12.1	+2.6
Ireland	70.2	70.2	0.0	13.5	7.8	−5.7	16.3	22.0	+5.7
Netherlands	75.6	78.1	+2.5	5.2	3.2	−2.0	19.2	18.7	−0.5
EU 15	75.0	70.5	−4.5	7.2	7.3	+0.1	17.8	22.2	+4.6
	Women								
Austria	52.1	59.5	+7.4	1.8	3.3	+1.5	46.1	37.2	−8.9
Denmark	69.3	71.1	+1.8	6.5	5.7	−0.8	24.2	23.2	−0.1
Ireland	32.1	45.3	+13.2	7.4	5.1	+2.3	60.5	49.6	−10.9
Netherlands	39.5	54.9	+15.4	4.4	4.3	−0.1	56.1	40.8	−15.3
EU 15	45.0	50.5	+5.5	5.9	7.3	+1.4	49.1	42.2	−6.9

Source: Eurostat: *Community Labour Force Survey.*

the ranking of unemployment rates related to the population of working age, followed by the Netherlands, Denmark and Ireland. (That is the same rank order as in 1997 when standardized rates were 4.4 per cent for Austria, 5.2 per cent for the Netherlands, 6.1 per cent for Denmark and 10.2 per cent for Ireland). In trend terms, Ireland has had the strongest decline in unemployment rates, followed by Denmark and the Netherlands. Austria has even seen a slight increase in this rate, but from a low level. While Austria and Denmark both have adjusted (i.e. in full-time equivalents) and non-adjusted employment rates that are higher than the EU average, Ireland has lower rates in both dimensions. The Netherlands has higher non-adjusted rates, but falls below the EU average once working time is taken into account.

Employment rates calculated in full-time equivalents (FTE) show that both Ireland and the Netherlands have almost equally low rates, while the difference between Austria and Denmark shrinks to a mere 3.5 percentage points (see table 2.2). Differences between employment rates expressed per capita and FTE rates are explained by differences in working time, and especially between the incidence of full- and part-time jobs. The Netherlands has the highest part-time shares in the EU, and Denmark also shows high

Table 2.2. Full-time equivalent employment rates, 1985 and 1997, and changes, 1985–97 (as percentage of total population aged 15–64)

Country	1985	1997	Change 1985–97
		Men and women	
Austria	63.2	65.0	+1.8
Denmark	67.2	68.5	+1.3
Ireland	49.6	53.7	+3.9
Netherlands	47.2	53.0	+5.8
EU 15	55.6	55.0	−0.6
		Men	
Austria	81.6	78.9	−2.7
Denmark	78.9	77.1	−1.8
Ireland	69.4	68.1	−1.3
Netherlands	69.1	71.1	+2.0
EU 15	73.5	68.3	−5.2
		Women	
Austria	46.2	51.5	+5.3
Denmark	54.5	60.3	+5.8
Ireland	29.6	39.8	+10.2
Netherlands	25.8	35.1	+9.3
EU 15	38.6	42.2	+3.6

Source: European Commission: *Employment in Europe*, 1998.

rates, while Austria has a low share of part-time jobs. In Denmark FTE rates increased more than non-adjusted rates because of a halt in the expansion of part-time jobs, resulting in markedly more women working full time today than in 1985.

EMPLOYMENT RATES IN DETAIL

A more detailed look at the non-adjusted employment rates reveals varying degrees of participation of the working-age population, not only across countries but also according to sex, age and education.[1] For the European Commission employment rates have now become the most important success indicator, as an increase in the employment rate should be the main outcome of the European Employment Strategy. As table 2.1 shows, Denmark has by far the highest rates both for women and men. The high rate for women is exceptional – for example it is around 26 percentage points higher than the Irish rate. Differences for men are less marked, especially between Denmark, Austria and the Netherlands.

Employment rates have increased most in Ireland and the Netherlands, while they have risen moderately in Austria and stabilized at a high level in Denmark. In general, the increase in employment rates has been higher for

7

Table 2.3. Employment rates[1] by age group, 1985 and 1997

Age group	Austria		Denmark		Ireland		Netherlands		European Union	
	1985	1997	1985	1997	1985	1997	1985	1997	1985	1997
15–24	64.2	55.7	68.4	69.4	43.3	38.4	49.0	55.8	44.3	35.9
25–54	79.3	82.5	84.7	84.4	55.1	67.8	66.7	76.3	71.1	73.2
55–64	28.6	29.3	51.2	52.2	41.1	40.2	28.5	30.7	38.0	35.9
Total	67.3	70.0	77.4	77.5	51.4	57.9	57.7	66.7	60.0	60.5

Note: [1] Employment as a share of the working-age population in corresponding age brackets.
Source: European Commission: *Employment Rates Report*, 1998.

women, while male rates have fallen in Austria and Denmark, stabilized in Ireland and even increased in the Netherlands.

Employment rates by age group show a divergent picture (see table 2.3). Two countries have increased the employment participation of youth (Denmark, the Netherlands), while the other two (Austria, Ireland) have lower youth employment rates today than in 1985. For Austria and Ireland the decline in employment rates reflects an increase in the participation of youth in full-time education (for Austria there is also a decrease in the numbers of apprentices, who were counted as employed). However, the increase in the Netherlands and Denmark does not reflect lower participation in education, but an increase in the (relative) number of young people combining education and training with work. This is the case in the Netherlands, where the share of those combining education and training with work has risen from only 10 per cent in 1983 to around 50 per cent in 1995. This is partly the consequence of a reduction in study grants, but is helped greatly by the availability of part-time jobs (Auer, 1998).

With the exception of Denmark, the prime-age groups (25–54) have seen their employment rates increasing everywhere, particularly in Ireland and the Netherlands. Except for Ireland, the employment rate for the older age groups (55–64) has increased slightly over the period, reflecting an increase in the employment rates of women and a decrease in inflows into early retirement schemes, which affected men in particular.

Table 2.4 shows the difference between male and female employment rates for the four countries over time. Over the period as a whole, the gender gap is highest in Ireland and the Netherlands, and lowest in Denmark. However, the reduction in the gender gap has also been highest in Ireland and the Netherlands, followed by Austria. Differences are lowest between young men and women and highest between older men and women. Thus it seems that the structural effects of the labour markets are strong, but that trends are clearly towards a reduction in the gap as younger cohorts join and progress

Table 2.4. Gender gap in employment rates by age[1], 1985 and 1997

Age group	Austria		Denmark		Ireland		Netherlands	
	1985	1997	1985	1997	1985	1997	1985	1997
15–24	−7.3	−7.8	−8.4	−9.1	−4.9	−5.2	−7.5	−4.7
25–54	−37.8	−22.3	−11.6	−12.0	−48.4	−29.0	−45.3	−26.9
55–64	−33.6	−25.0	−22.7	−10.2	−48.6	−37.7	−32.5	−23.6
Total	−31.0	−20.9	−14.9	−12.8	−38.1	−25.2	−35.7	−23.2

Note: [1] Differences in male/female employment rates in percentage points.
Sources: European Commission: *Employment Rates Report*, 1998; author's calculations.

through the labour market. The slight increase in the youth gap (except in the Netherlands, where the gap has narrowed) seems to be due to higher participation of young women in education and training rather than to employment discrimination (European Commission, 1998d).

For the prime age groups, moderate male increases in the employment rate (except for Austria) go together with strong female increases (except for Denmark). For the older age group the declining gap results both from a (sometimes strong) decline in male employment due to early retirement and an increase in female employment.

Employment rates differ not only by sex and age, but also by education and marital status.

Table 2.5 is straightforward: employment rates rise with educational level both for men and women, and the gender gap is narrowest for those with higher (tertiary) education and widest for those with less than upper secondary education. In other words, the more skills the labour force acquires, the lower will be the gaps between the employment rates of men and women. Education can therefore be seen as a major driving force for equal opportunities, at least as far as access to employment is concerned.

Table 2.5. Employment rates by level of education, 1994

Level of education	Austria			Denmark			Ireland			Netherlands		
	M	F	M-F	M	F	M-F	M	F	M-F	M	F	M-F
Low	70.0	47.0	23.0	65.7	55.5	10.2	67.0	24.4	42.6	70.6	36.2	34.4
Mid	83.9	65.5	18.4	82.1	77.1	4.0	85.3	51.9	33.4	83.7	61.4	22.3
High	91.6	84.7	6.9	89.3	87.8	1.5	90.2	74.3	15.9	87.0	74.9	12.1

Source: ILO CEPR data bank.

Table 2.6. Employment rates by NACE 2-digit service sector (as percentage of working-age population)

Sector	Austria	Denmark	Ireland	Netherlands	France	Germany	United Kingdom	United States	EU15	E15-US
Distribution	11.0	10.4	8.2	11.0	8.1	8.8	11.0	12.1	9.1	−3.0
Hotels and restaurants	4.0	2.3	3.2	2.2	2.0	2.0	3.3	5.4	2.0	−2.9
Transport and communication	4.4	5.5	2.7	4.0	3.8	3.3	4.6	4.1	3.6	−0.5
Finance and insurance	2.7	2.6	2.1	2.4	1.9	2.2	3.1	3.3	2.1	−1.2
Business services	4.6	6.2	3.6	7.0	5.2	4.3	7.0	7.8	4.6	−3.2
Communal services, of which:	17.6	27.3	15.2	22.3	20.4	17.8	21.4	21.4	17.8	−3.4
Public administration	4.8	4.8	3.1	5.3	5.6	5.5	4.3	3.3	4.7	+1.4
Education	4.1	5.8	3.8	4.3	4.5	3.3	5.3	5.7	4.1	−1.6
Health and social work	5.5	13.0	5.0	9.5	6.3	5.7	7.8	8.4	5.7	−2.7

Source: European Commission: *Employment Rates Report*, 1998.

Women's employment rates are also influenced by marital status and parenthood. The four countries vary with respect to the type of household. Danish women have high employment rates independent of marital status, with even slightly higher rates for married women. The fact of having children does not affect female rates in Denmark dramatically. In Ireland, the Netherlands, and to a lesser extent also in Austria, single and married women also have similar employment rates, but the fact of having children or not leads to more pronounced differences. In 1997 the differences in employment rates of married over single women aged 30 to 39 were as follows: Austria −8.1 percentage points, the Netherlands −3.1 points and Ireland −3.8 points; if single and married mothers with children (below age 5) are compared with women without children, differences are around 20 points in the Netherlands and Austria, and around 40 points in Ireland. With regard to working mothers, Ireland and Denmark are therefore at opposing ends: having a child does not induce women to withdraw from the labour market in Denmark, because of the availability of childcare facilities and parental leave. In Ireland, mothers more often stay at home in the absence of these. This is, of course, to some extent a statistical artefact, as parental leave in Denmark maintains the employment relationship. While in Austria and the Netherlands married mothers have lower employment rates than single mothers, in Ireland single mothers have lower rates than married mothers. Employment rates decline with the number of children and rise with the age of children, again differently by country. It can also be seen that women's employment rates have risen independently of marital and parenthood status (on this point see Rubery, forthcoming).

Differences in the service sector account for many of the differences in employment rates between the countries. Table 2.6 shows that Denmark and the Netherlands have high relative employment rates both in business and in communal services, while Austria and Ireland have markedly lower rates. Danish rates are especially high in health and social work, as well as in education (the two items explain about 80 per cent of the 10 percentage point difference in employment rates between Denmark and Austria). Most of the rest is explained by differences in business services. The Netherlands has also comparatively high rates (above American levels) in health and social work, as well as in business services.

Differences between the United States and Europe are also particularly strong in health and social work, business services, distribution (retail trade) and financial services (insurance).

EMPLOYMENT

Over a period of 16 years (1980–96) the four countries have had very dissimilar employment growth rates. On annual averages between 1980 and 1996, employment grew by 1.2 per cent in Austria, 0.4 per cent in Denmark,

Table 2.7. Recent employment growth: Average annual growth rates, 1992–98 (percentages)

Country	1992–97	1997	1998
Austria	0.95	0.2	0.5
Denmark	0.71	2.7	2.2
Ireland	3.63	5.0	6.9
Netherlands	1.47	2.8	2.7

Source: European Commission: *Joint Employment Report*, 1998, 1999.

0.8 per cent in Ireland and 2.1 per cent in the Netherlands. However, fluctuating periods of strong and weak employment growth lead to changes in rankings over time. For example, in the economic upswing of 1985 to 1989, Denmark had higher employment growth rates than Austria, while employment in Ireland was actually declining. The Netherlands still had the highest employment growth rates. In the following period, 1990 to 1994, Austria together with Ireland had the highest rates (2.2 per cent), followed by the Netherlands with 1.7 per cent. In this period, Denmark actually suffered a 0.7 per cent decline in employment. Recent figures taken from the European Union's *Joint Employment Report*, 1998 and 1999, covering the period 1992 to 1998, are shown in table 2.7.

These divergent trends show the importance of the time dimension in comparing countries: employment growth varies over time, and countries change places in rankings and are not successful in all periods. Austria has been rather successful in the longer-term perspective, but not very recently. For Denmark and Ireland the opposite holds true: while these countries are only moderately successful in the long term, they have been very successful recently, with high employment growth rates, especially in Ireland. The Netherlands has been successful both in the long and the short term. Compared to the EU as a whole, only Denmark has a lower than average growth rate in the longer term (16 years), while the other countries have had higher employment growth rates. Recently Ireland, the Netherlands and Denmark have had employment growth rates far above the EU average, which in 1997 was only 0.53 per cent, owing to low growth or even falling employment in Germany, France and Italy.

The gender situation

Over the 16 years from 1980 to 1996 the increase in women's employment was larger than that for men in all countries (table 2.8). This holds true both in the long term and the short term for the Netherlands and Ireland. The short-term performance of women (1995–96) is not as positive in Austria and Denmark, although both countries have relatively high employment rates for both men

Table 2.8. Employment growth by sex, 1980–96 and 1995–96

Country	1980–96[1]		1995–96[2]	
	Male	Female	Male	Female
Austria	12.6	34.1	−0.3	−0.45
Denmark[3]	7.6	11.9	1.7	1.0
Ireland	−1.7	52.3	3.0	5.9
Netherlands	16.9	88.5	2.2	2.5

Notes: [1] Percentage change 1980–96. [2] Annual average change. [3] 1981–96.
Source: ILO CEPR database.

and women. As well as employment levels, the structure of employment is also important, as it reveals at least some of the quality aspects of employment created.

The structural dimensions covered here are: employment creation by sector and firm size, by dependent and independent work, by private and public jobs, by full- and part-time employment, and by permanent and fixed-term contracts. Unfortunately, all these figures are available only as stocks, and do not show, for example, the number of jobs created on a fixed-term basis, but transformed into permanent jobs within the year.

The sectoral distribution of employment

Both the Netherlands and Denmark have a high share of employment in the service sector (table 2.9). The difference between these two countries and Austria and Ireland is around 10 percentage points. Austria and Ireland still have the largest shares of employment in industry and in agriculture. Agricultural employment remains particularly high in Ireland. In all countries the proportion of women in services is far higher than that of men, while the proportion of men in industry is much higher. This traditional segmentation of jobs is especially visible in the Netherlands, where less than 10 per cent of women work in industry. A high share of women in industry (as in Ireland) goes together with a high share of total employment in industry.

The shifts in favour of the service sector have been strongest in the two countries, Austria and Ireland, with the greatest need to catch up in terms of structural change. Except for Ireland, industrial employment has continued to shrink everywhere. In Ireland, while services have grown most strongly, industrial employment has also recovered in the 1990s. According to national sources, it grew at an annual rate of 3 per cent between 1991 and 1997, mainly in the foreign-owned manufacturing sector (O'Connell, 1999).

Service subsectors such as finance and business, and communal services showed the highest growth rates (see also table 2.6).

Table 2.9.   Wage and salary earners by sector, 1996 (as percentage of total)

Sector	Austria	Denmark	Ireland	Netherlands	EU 15
Agriculture/fishing	**1.2**	**2.1**	**2.7**	**1.6**	**1.9**
Mining/quarrying	0.3	0.2	0.5	0.1	0.5
Manufacturing	23.5	19.8	21.8	16.6	22.8
Electricity, gas, water	1.1	0.8	1.3	0.7	1.0
Construction	8.5	6.3	7.2	5.8	7.2
Total industry	**33.4**	**27.1**	**30.8**	**23.3**	**31.5**
Trade	16.3	12.8	13.8	15.6	13.4
Hotels/restaurants	4.7	2.6	5.4	2.8	3.4
Transport, communication	7.4	7.1	4.7	6.4	6.3
Financial services	3.9	3.5	4.7	3.6	3.9
Other business services	6.2	6.3	6.3	8.9	6.7
Public administration	7.6	6.9	7.2	8.3	9.2
Other services	19.4	31.4	24.4	24.4	23.5
Total services	**65.5**	**70.6**	**66.6**	**70.1**	**66.4**
Total	**100.0**	**100.0**	**100.0**	**100.0**	**100.0**

Source: Eurostat: *European Labour Force Survey Results*, 1996.

Employment by company size

The service sector (except for public services) is largely composed of smaller establishments and firms. Employment growth in this sector should therefore also mean a more than proportionate growth in small and medium-sized enterprises (SMEs). In the literature, the contribution of SMEs to employment creation has often been emphasized, and indeed, in all of the countries under review, SMEs play a crucial role in employment.

Table 2.10 shows that in Denmark, Austria and Ireland SMEs in all sectors of the economy account for over 60 per cent of total employment. In Denmark, as much as over 70 per cent of the workforce is employed in such firms. In Ireland, large firms have a slightly bigger share of employment than SMEs. If we abstract from the dynamics of job creation, and look only at changes in size distribution over time as a proxy for net job changes, we may conclude that SMEs' contribution to net employment change has not varied dramatically in the last ten years. However, the contribution to employment by SMEs, even with a constant size distribution over the decade, is of the order of 60–70 per cent of all jobs. Only in Ireland has slightly less than 50 per cent of employment been created in SMEs. It can be shown also that the two countries with the most impressive recent job creation record, Ireland and the Netherlands, have had the largest, but still only modest increases in the share of SMEs (table 2.10). Size distribution effects arise also from the fact that these two countries have created overwhelmingly private sector jobs, whereas both Austria and Denmark have created many public sector jobs.

Table 2.10. Employment by company size, 1988 and 1997 (percentages)

Country	Very small (1)	Small (2)	Medium (3)	(1)–(3)	Large (4)
Austria					
1988	24.5	19.0	21.2	64.6	35.4
1997	25.0	18.8	20.7	64.5	35.5
Denmark					
1988	29.9	22.5	18.1	70.5	29.5
1997	29.8	22.2	18.0	70.0	30.0
Ireland					
1988	18.6	16.6	13.5	48.7	51.3
1997	18.6	16.3	14.6	49.4	50.6
Netherlands					
1988	25.2	18.7	15.6	59.5	40.5
1997	26.1	19.0	15.2	60.4	39.6

Notes: (1) Less than 10 employees; (2) 10 to 50; (3) 50 to 250; (4) over 500.
Source: European Observatory for SMEs: *Fifth Annual Report*, 1997.

Private and public sector employment

Table 2.11 shows the distribution of private and public sector jobs created over the period 1980–96. It appears that, in the Netherlands, on balance only private sector jobs were created, while the number of public sector jobs stagnated. In Ireland, overwhelmingly private sector jobs were created whereas the contrary happened in Austria, where private sector jobs contracted, while public sector jobs expanded. Denmark created more jobs in the private than in the public sector, but public sector job creation was considerable.

Table 2.11, which presents figures for the United Kingdom and France, shows convincingly the results of two opposed processes: government

Table 2.11. Growth of private and public sector employment in various EU countries, 1980–96

Total employment (1980–96)	Index (1980 = 100)	Change ('000)	Private sector[1] ('000)	Public sector ('000)
Austria	104.4	143	−65	208
Denmark	108.9	211	120	91
France	102.0	441	−663	1 104
Ireland	111.5	136	107	29
Netherlands	119.3	999	997	2
Sweden	93.6	−270	−235	−35
United Kingdom	105.2	1 312	3 012	−1 700

Note: [1] Self-employed are included.
Source: Pichelmann (with Hofer), 1999.

reduction and retreat in the United Kingdom versus expansion of public jobs in France. In a way, Austria has gone along the French path, while the Netherlands has taken the British road without, however, reducing public sector jobs, but rather merely stabilizing them. Ireland and Denmark are in between the two extreme cases, with Denmark more similar to Austria and Ireland more similar to the Netherlands.

Self-employment and dependent employment

As table 2.12 shows, the overall share of self-employment has grown only in the Netherlands, but not in the other three countries. However, this has much to do with a still declining agricultural sector in these three countries, as many operatives in this sector are in fact independent farmers. National data for Ireland show this convincingly: according to this source, from 1981 to 1995 total self-employment increased by around 8 per cent. If agriculture (which counted for 62 per cent of all self-employed in 1981, and 58 per cent in 1996) is excluded, growth rates for non-agricultural self-employment are 65 per cent, much stronger than for dependent employment (O'Connell, 1999). Also in the Netherlands, self-employment in non-agricultural sectors (mainly services) has risen. In this regard, the European Commission's labour market report for the Netherlands notes that between 1987 and 1990 self-employment rose less than dependent employment, whereas it rose more strongly than dependent employment between 1990 and 1994. The authors conclude that growth in self-employment seems to be negatively correlated with economic growth (EC, 1997). Such a push factor for self-employment (because of a shortage of jobs as an alternative to unemployment) is also mentioned in O'Connell (1999). However, pull factors are also at work and self-employment cannot be seen only as an alternative to job shortages, but corresponds also to changed preferences. In Austria self-employment in sectors other than agriculture has risen only very marginally and has not

Table 2.12.   Shares of self-employment in total employment, 1985 and 1997

Country	Total			Men			Women		
	1985	1997	+/−	1985	1997	+/−	1985	1997	+/−
Austria	11.3	10.8	−0.5	12.4	12.6	+0.2	9.7	8.4	−1.3
Denmark	9.9	8.3	−1.6	15.2	12.1	−3.1	3.3	3.7	+0.4
Ireland	21.5	19.5	−2.0	27.8	27.0	−0.8	7.4	7.5	+0.1
Netherlands	9.1	11.3	+2.2	11.6	13.4	+1.8	4.3	8.3	+4.0
EU 15	15.2	14.9	−0.3	18.8	18.8	0.0	9.3	9.5	+0.2

Source: Eurostat (including agriculture).

offset the declining trend of agricultural self-employment. Danish figures point to similar developments.

In conclusion, in the countries with the highest rates of overall employment growth (and also private sector employment) self-employment in the non-agricultural sectors, and in particular in the service sector, was an important contributory factor to employment growth (e.g. accounting for around 14 per cent of Irish job growth between 1981 and 1996).

Part-time and full-time employment

We now turn to the question of whether an expansion of part-time jobs is linked to employment growth in some of the countries under review (table 2.13). In particular, the Netherlands has a high part-time share (defined here as those working less than 30 hours a week): almost 30 per cent of the labour force worked part time in 1997. Denmark comes second with about 18 per cent, closely followed by Ireland with around 17 per cent. In Austria, only about 11 per cent of the unemployed work part time. While the part-time share has been rather stable in Austria over the last four years, it increased strongly in Ireland and more moderately in the Netherlands, and actually even declined in Denmark.

Part-time rates for men are considerably lower than for women. Austria has not only the lowest, but also declining rates among men. The Netherlands too has low and declining rates for men, whereas male part-time rates have risen considerably in Denmark and Ireland. With the exception of the Netherlands, where they are remarkably higher than in any other country, female rates are rather similar among the three remaining countries. They are strongly declining in Denmark, however, indicating that there could be a threshold at which women demand full-time rather than part-time jobs. If so, such a threshold could also have been reached in the Netherlands, with a female part-time share of around 55 per cent, as the share of women in part-time jobs declined

Table 2.13. Part-time shares in total employment, 1994 and 1997 (less than 30 hours per week)

Country	Total			Men			Women		
	1994	1997	1994/97	1994	1997	1994/97	1994	1997	1994/97
Austria	10.6	10.8	0.2	2.3	2.1	−0.2	21.6	22.0	0.4
Denmark	18.0	17.9	−0.1	10.2	11.9	1.7	26.7	24.7	−2.0
Ireland	14.8	16.7	1.9	4.2	5.1	0.9	24.7	27.1	2.4
Netherlands	28.4	29.1	0.7	10.7	10.6	−0.1	53.5	54.6	1.1

Sources: OECD: *Employment Outlook*, 1998; author's calculations.

Table 2.14. Part-time shares in total employment, 1985 and 1997 (less than 35 hours per week)

Country	Total			Men			Women		
	1985	1997	+/−	1985	1997	+/−	1985	1997	+/−
Austria	11.1	14.9	+3.8	3.4	4.0	+0.6	23.1	29.0	+5.9
Denmark	24.3	22.2	−2.1	8.4	12.1	+3.7	43.9	34.5	−9.4
Ireland	6.5	12.3	+5.8	2.4	5.4	+3.0	15.5	23.2	+7.7
Netherlands	22.7	38.0	+15.3	13.8	17.0	+3.2	57.5	67.9	+10.4
EU 15	12.7	16.9	+4.2	3.7	5.8	+2.1	28.0	32.4	+4.4

Source: Eurostat.

between 1996 and 1997. In general, part-time work is strongly gender biased, with women accounting for between 90 per cent of all part-time jobs in Austria and 65 per cent in Denmark. In the Netherlands the share is around 80 per cent, and in Ireland around 75 per cent. While in the other countries the differences between women's and men's part-time rates are in the order of 10:1 (Austria) or 5:1 (Ireland, the Netherlands), they are only around 2:1 in Denmark.

If we define part-time shares in terms of those working less than 35 hours per week (table 2.14), part-time shares and growth rates are even higher. Thus defined, an increasing number of men work part time in all four countries. It is probable, however, that these figures also include men who work a reduced full-time week (e.g. shift work).

Returning to our initial question of the contribution of part-time work to employment growth, table 2.15 shows that in the Netherlands around 80 per cent and in Ireland around 50 per cent of all jobs created between 1989 and 1994 were part time, whereas they also accounted for more than

Table 2.15. Contributions of full-time and part-time jobs to net job change, 1989–94 (percentages)

Country	Male		Female		Total
	Full-time	Part-time	Full-time	Part-time	
Denmark	−2.3	0.1	1.7	−3.1	−3.6
Ireland	0.6	1.5	4.6	3.5	10.2
Netherlands	1.9	1.2	0.7	7.7	11.5
EU 12	−2.1	0.6	0.4	2.0	0.8

Note: No data are available for Austria.
Source: Rubery et al. (1999), on the basis of the *European Labour Force Survey*.

80 per cent of all jobs lost in Denmark during that time. Table 2.14 suggests that part-time work was further on the increase, in particular in Ireland (where, however, lately more full-time jobs have been created) and the Netherlands, but also in Austria. Part-time work has also made a recent comeback in Denmark as well, but mainly for men.

Part-time work has many facets, and ranges from voluntarily reduced full-time work to involuntary marginal part-time work. In 1996, both in the Netherlands and Denmark around 30 per cent of all part-time jobs were for less than ten hours a week. Such marginal part-time work affected men much more than women. The figures are 10 per cent for Austria and 17 per cent for Ireland. While part-time work seems to be largely voluntary in the Netherlands (70 per cent claim that they did not want full-time work) and also in Denmark (for around 50 per cent of part-time workers), for around 30 per cent of the Irish part-timers the choice to work part time was made because of the absence of suitable full-time work. This figure for male part-timers was even higher, at over 55 per cent. Again, we are in the presence of push (lack of alternatives, family situation, health impairment, etc.) and pull factors (change of lifestyle, value placed on leisure) which are behind the rise in part-time jobs.

Part-time work seems important for job growth, and is, for example, part and parcel of Dutch employment growth. With increasing part-time employment (which often is also of a temporary nature), it is desirable that conditions of employment with regard to pay, social protection and working conditions are at least on a pro-rata basis with full-time work. In particular, social protection schemes offering a basic pension (usually topped up by a contribution-based system, as in Denmark and the Netherlands) might be one of the necessary conditions for allowing the development of part-time work. Recent changes in the Dutch legislation, which allow the building up of decent old-age pensions, despite heterogeneous employment careers, seem to be promising answers to modern employment patterns. "Bismarckian", contribution-based pension systems create disincentives for taking up part-time work, as they result in forgone earnings during retirement.

Permanent and fixed-term employment

Fixed-term employment now affects around 8 to 11 per cent of the labour force, and between 1985 and 1997 it increased by around 50 per cent in the Netherlands and around 30 per cent in Ireland, but declined in Denmark (table 2.16). Women usually account for a higher share of fixed-term employment than men. Gender differences range from around 70 per cent in the Netherlands and Ireland to around 15 per cent in Austria and under 10 per cent in Denmark. While the fixed-term share is not particularly significant in stock terms, it is more important in flow terms (Schömann et al., 1998). Even a weakly increasing stock of fixed-term contracts might hide an increasing

Table 2.16.   Share of fixed-term contracts in total employment, 1985 and 1997

Country	Men			Women			Total		
	1985	1997	+/−	1985	1997	+/−	1985	1997	+/−
Austria	n.a.	7.3	n.a.	n.a.	8.4	n.a.	n.a.	7.8	n.a.
Denmark	11.6	10.6	−1.0	13.1	11.6	−1.5	12.3	11.1	−0.8
Ireland	5.5	7.1	+1.6	10.6	12.1	+1.5	7.3	9.4	+2.1
Netherlands	5.9	8.8	+2.9	10.8	14.9	+4.1	7.5	11.4	+3.9
EU 15	7.5	11.5	+4.0	9.7	13.1	+3.4	8.4	12.2	+3.8

n.a. = not available.
Source: Eurostat: *European Labour Force Surveys*, several years.

share of fixed-term contracts in flow terms, that is, among new contracts. In such a case, fixed-term employment acts as a bridge into the labour market and while it might be used to prolong probationary periods, most fixed-term employment contracts are, at the end of the day, transformed into permanent contracts (about 90 per cent in all countries). Fixed-term contracts are inversely related to age, and thus largely affect young people.

This implies that, while fixed-term contracts might be playing an increasing role in European employment systems, their actual extent is often exaggerated, and they may act as a bridge into the labour market. Some reforms in the legal coverage of this form of employment have already been undertaken. The most promising is the Dutch "flexicurity" approach, which obliges temporary work agencies to offer permanent contracts to their contract workers after two years of service. In the Netherlands temporary agencies also engage in training their staff and have contractual relationships with the public employment service for such training and placement activities. These new developments seem to lead to a new labour market segment of flexible but protected workers. This is not to say that other forms of temporary work, which are often at the same time also part-time work, are not to be considered "precarious" and in need of some regulation in the sense of "flexicurity". For example, in some countries (e.g. Austria) unprotected work below the social security threshold has developed, and Hartog (1999) shows, for the Netherlands, that there are many new forms of flexible employment which are not reflected in the official statistics. There are unfortunately no comparative statistics allowing the relative dimensions of voluntary and involuntary fixed-term contracts to be measured, but a large proportion of them can be assumed to be involuntary.

UNEMPLOYMENT

Unemployment rates have attracted much attention as a major indicator of labour market problems. No wonder, then, that the reduction in unemployment

Figure 2.1.   Unemployment rates, 1980–98

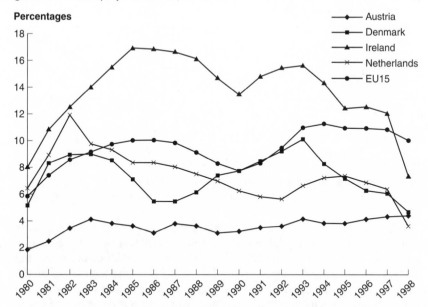

Notes: Labour Force Concept (ILO). Data for 1998 are seasonally adjusted for November 1998.
Source: Eurostat.

is seen as the major achievement of the countries under review. Only Austria has recently experienced a rise in unemployment, but still has low (and presently declining) rates and a long-standing record in terms of low unemployment rates.[2]

Seen over the long term it appears that the recent achievements are considerable (figure 2.1). Unemployment soared in particular following the second oil crisis at the beginning of the 1980s and again in the recession of the early 1990s. Peaks in rates differ across countries and over time: the Netherlands reached its unemployment peak in 1982 (almost 12 per cent), Ireland in 1985 (17 per cent) and Denmark as late as 1993 (more than 10 per cent), while Austria experienced rather stable rates at the relatively low level of around 4 per cent throughout the period.

If we compare these peaks with very recent seasonally adjusted figures, the extent of the achievement is indeed impressive.

Table 2.17 shows that with the exception of Austria, which has experienced a slight increase in unemployment over this very recent period, the three other countries have reduced their unemployment rates considerably. In particular, in March 1999, male unemployment in the Netherlands reached less than 3 per cent, the level – according to Beveridge – corresponding to full employment.

Table 2.17. Unemployment change, March 1997/March 1999, seasonally adjusted (percentage points)

Country	Male			Female			Total			Gender gap
	March 1997	March 1999	Change	March 1997	March 1999	Change	March 1997	March 1999	Change	March 1999
Austria	3.6	3.8	+0.2	5.2	5.4	+0.2	4.3	4.6	+0.3	1.6
Denmark	4.8	3.7	−1.1	6.9	5.7	−1.2	5.8	4.7	−1.1	2.0
Ireland	10.4	6.9	−3.5	10.7	6.9	−3.8	10.5	6.9	−3.6	0.0
Netherlands	4.2	2.6	−1.8	7.0	4.9	−2.1	7.0	3.6	−3.4	2.3
EU 15	9.5	8.2	−1.3	12.4	11.3	−1.1	10.7	9.6	−1.1	1.7

Sources: European Commission: Eurostat press release 4299/6.5.99.

In a simple EU ranking, the Netherlands now has the second lowest unemployment rates after Luxembourg, followed almost on a par by Austria and Denmark. Forecasts show that the reduction in unemployment is to continue and that even Austria has again enjoyed declining rates in the first half of 1999. Ireland, while having considerably reduced its unemployment levels, still suffers from high unemployment and in particular from long-term unemployment.

The reduction in unemployment is partly due to economic growth and employment creation, which were particularly strong in the Netherlands and in Ireland, and recently also in Denmark. Schettkat (forthcoming) shows increased Okun coefficients (measuring the impact of growth on unemployment) for three of the countries, while Austria's low rate is explained less by the impact of growth on unemployment than by a highly reactive labour supply.

The gender gap in unemployment

Male and female unemployment developed differently over time and across countries. In Ireland, it was consistently higher for men until the downturn of the early 1990s, which affected women disproportionately. By contrast, it was consistently higher for women than for men in Denmark, Ireland and Austria. Recently (March 1997 to March 1999), in Ireland, Denmark and the Netherlands women's unemployment has been decreasing more rapidly than men's, while it increased proportionally in Austria. Gender gaps in unemployment were thus either reduced or remained stable (table 2.17). Gender gaps are much higher in the EU as a whole, and especially in Italy and France.

Long-term unemployment

A comparison of the reduction of total unemployment and long-term unemployment between 1992 and 1997 suggests that it is almost proportional

Table 2.18. Long-term unemployment (LTU) rates, 1992–98, and incidence, 1991–97

Country	LTU rate			Incidence (LTU/total unemployed)		
	1992	1998	1992/98 (% points)	1991	1997	1991/97
Austria	n.a.	1.5	n.a.	n.a.	28.5	n.a.
Denmark	2.4	1.4	−1.0	35	27.2	−7.8
Ireland	8.7	5.7	−3.0	62.6	56.6	−5.9
Netherlands	2.4	1.9	−0.5	43.9	49.2	+5.3
EU	n.a.	4.9	n.a.	47.6	49.0	+1.4

n.a. = not available.
Sources: European Commission: *Joint Employment Report*, 1998, 1999; *Employment in Europe*, 1998, 1999.

in Ireland and Denmark, as is the increase in Austria. If we consider only the change between 1996 and 1997, similar reductions in long-term unemployment and total unemployment also occurred in the Netherlands. Table 2.18, which also compares long-term unemployment incidence over time, suggests that long-term unemployment actually declined more rapidly than total unemployment in Denmark and Ireland. Older workers account for a disproportionate number of the long-term unemployed, but there seems to be some substitution with other exit measures such as early retirement or invalidity pension schemes, which have contributed to lower unemployment levels for older workers. Low educational levels and health impairment are other factors increasing the risk of long-term unemployment. One of the major risk factors is a prior prolonged period of unemployment (the so-called hysteresis effect).

In 1997 the long-term unemployment rate in three countries was slightly higher for women than for men; gender gaps are 1.3 percentage points in the Netherlands, 0.6 in Denmark and 0.1 in Austria. Only in Ireland was there a positive gender gap for women, who had a long-term unemployment rate that was 1.8 percentage points lower than that for men.

Youth unemployment

Youth unemployment is a particularly important problem, as any society should avoid young people starting working life with experience of an unemployment period. Youth unemployment rates have usually been higher than adult rates in all the countries under review (table 2.19).

The youth gap (the difference between youth and adult rates) in 1997 was 2.3 percentage points in Austria, 2.1 in Denmark, 4 in the Netherlands and 5.8 in Ireland. The gap slightly improved from its 1990 level in Austria and Ireland, notably improved in Denmark, but worsened in the Netherlands, at

Table 2.19. Youth unemployment rates, 1990–97 (percentage of labour force aged 15–24)

Country	1990			1997		
	Male	Female	Total	Male	Female	Total
Austria	4.5	8.0	6.2	5.6	7.8	6.7
Denmark	11.3	11.5	11.4	6.7	9.9	8.2
Ireland	20.4	18.2	19.4	16.5	15.3	16.0
Netherlands	7.5	9.6	8.6	8.1	10.4	9.2
EU	13.9	17.5	15.6	19.5	22.8	21.0

Source: European Commission: *Employment in Europe*, 1998.

least until 1997. Except for Ireland, young women have higher unemployment rates than men.

Very recent figures show that youth unemployment has started to fall dramatically over the past two years, and by August 1998 was down to 6.4 per cent in the Netherlands, 6.5 per cent in Austria, 12.9 in Ireland and 6.8 in Denmark. This means that in Denmark and the Netherlands the youth gap has narrowed further.

Table 2.20. Unemployment rates by educational attainment, 1994 and 1995

Country	1994				1995			
	Less than upper secondary education	Upper secondary education	Tertiary-level education	Total	Less than upper secondary education	Upper secondary education	Tertiary-level education	Total
Austria	4.9	2.8	1.7	3.6	5.7	2.9	1.8	3.7
Men	4.8	2.6	1.6	3.3	n.a.	n.a.	n.a.	3.2
Women	5.1	3.3	1.8	4.0	n.a.	n.a.	n.a.	4.3
Denmark	17.3	10.0	5.3	8.0	14.6	8.3	4.8	7.0
Men	16.3	9.3	5.5	7.1	n.a.	n.a.	n.a.	6.1
Women	18.4	10.9	5.0	9.0	n.a.	n.a.	n.a.	8.1
Ireland	18.9	9.7	4.9	14.7	16.4	7.6	4.2	12.1
Men	18.0	8.5	4.3	14.7	n.a.	n.a.	n.a.	12.2
Women	21.6	11.0	5.8	14.9	n.a.	n.a.	n.a.	12.1
Netherlands	8.2	4.8	4.3	6.8	7.9	4.8	4.1	7.1
Men	7.1	3.7	3.6	6.0	n.a.	n.a.	n.a.	5.9
Women	9.8	6.4	5.2	8.1	n.a.	n.a.	n.a.	8.7

n.a. = not available.
Notes: "Less than upper secondary education" corresponds to levels 0/1/2 of the International Standard Classification of Education (ISCED) classification; "upper secondary education" refers to ISCED level 3, while "tertiary education" includes levels 6/7 of the same classification.
Sources: OECD: *Education at a Glance*, various issues; *Labour Force Statistics*, 1976–96.

Unemployment by educational level

As employment rates rise with educational level, so unemployment rates fall. Table 2.20 shows the merit of education in helping avoid unemployment for all countries and both sexes. The message is straightforward: the higher the educational level, the lower the unemployment rate. While education offers no absolute guarantee against joblessness, it is a strong competitive advantage in a rationed job market.

Unemployed households

Growing attention is paid today to the household situation of the unemployed (Gregg and Wadsworth, 1998; OECD, 1998b; Rubery, forthcoming) because of the way it affects the labour supply of individuals. In particular, jobless households (those with nobody in work) are seen as an important problem, as they adversely affect welfare and, where some of the household members are children, will affect their perception of society. Even in successful countries, a significant proportion of the unemployed live in such households (table 2.21) – which often are low-income households.

Among the unemployed, prime-age men and older persons are particularly affected. A slight reduction in the shares of prime-age men in the Netherlands and in Ireland has occurred in the recent employment boom, but the problem remains serious. Gregg and Wadsworth (1998) even speak of a polarization, i.e. a parallel increase in double-earner households and jobless households.

Hidden unemployment

While unemployment is still a serious problem, it is often argued that it is only the tip of the iceberg, and that to adequately address the problem of joblessness, a "broad" unemployment rate should be calculated (see in particular various OECD country economic surveys). Such a rate includes several other dimensions such as active labour market measures, invalidity pensions and

Table 2.21. Share of the unemployed living in jobless households, 1996

Country	% of all unemployed
Austria	39
Denmark	n.a.
Ireland	51
Netherlands	42

n.a. = not available.
Source: OECD: *Employment Outlook*, 1998.

Table 2.22. Unemployment rates (1), unemployment rates in the absence of labour market policy (2) and "extended" unemployment rates (3), 1996

Country	(1)	(2)	(3)
Austria[1]	4.4	$(5.1)^2$	10.8
Denmark	6.9	11.7	20.5
Ireland	12.2	18.4	n.a.
Netherlands	6.3	7.3	15.6

Notes: [1]1995. [2]Estimation based on national sources.
Source: European Commission: *Employment Observatory Trends*, No. 30, Summer 1998.

early retirement, which all serve to reduce labour supply (for a discussion, see European Commission, 1998c).

Table 2.22 can be taken only as a rough approximation of the real dimension of "broad" unemployment. Depending on what is considered as "broad", the rate will vary. For example, according to an OECD definition the broad unemployment rate for the Netherlands in 1996 was around 27 per cent (and has risen dramatically from 7 per cent in 1970). By this definition, all employment schemes as well as early retirement, disability benefits and social assistance are included. What is problematic, however, is that from the point of view of defenders of the "broad" unemployment concept, each labour force status for 15–64 year-olds which is not official employment or unemployment is in fact "hidden" unemployment. However, this is not undisputed. In Chapter 3 we will show that the difference between the unemployment rate without considering active measures and the official labour force survey (LFS) unemployment rate – (1) and (2) in table 2.22 – can also be considered as a gross efficiency measure of active labour market policy. That is to say, it should be regarded as the unemployment-reducing effect of active labour market policy measures, that is, as an additional effort made by governments to curb unemployment.

Presenting this effort as a way to hide unemployment (as is implied in the OECD *Economic Survey* on the Netherlands, 1998a) may be valid for theoretical reasons, but also distorts the reality of the labour market. This also holds true for a large part of the invalidity pension system. Dutch estimates show that at least 50 per cent of those claiming invalidity pensions claim it on health grounds. These persons, at least, should not be considered as "hidden unemployed". For those who have been granted invalidity pensions on labour market grounds, the same arguments as for those on early retirement apply. Both systems have been heavily used to adjust employment levels to structural change, usually with the consent of both trade unions and employers, and the State. It was considered a "cushioned" way of exit from the labour market until the system ran into cost problems.

Ever since, governments have tried to restrict this form of exit, with varying results. In any case, the alternative to early retirement would have been mostly "uncushioned" exits and a marked increase in "non-hidden" unemployment for older workers. While some changes in the system (and especially in the way it is financed) are required, and firms should indeed keep their workforce longer in employment, simply abandoning it would increase hardship at the end of working life (see also "Inactivity", below). So hidden unemployment is an ill-defined concept and should include only discouraged workers and other categories which do not actively participate in the job market, but not those having a defined labour market status with a replacement income justified by age and on health grounds.

INACTIVITY

The above discussion leads on to the third labour market category that we consider in this synthesis report: the so-called "inactives". The word is somewhat misleading, because the inactives are in fact composed of those in education, those retired below age 65 (e.g. often for reasons of early retirement or invalidity), and other categories such as those staying at home for family reasons.

Table 2.1 above shows that between 1985 and 1997 the inactives have declined in relative terms in Austria, Ireland and the Netherlands, but have increased slightly in Denmark. However, the level of inactivity in Denmark is still by far the lowest among the four countries compared. Except for the Netherlands, inactivity is increasing for men, reflecting not only the trend towards early retirement, but also an increase in the time spent in education. Usually women's inactivity rates are declining strongly (except for Denmark), mirroring the increase in their employment rates.

Inactivity rates by age show divergent patterns (table 2.23). For the young, they have declined in both Denmark and the Netherlands, but have risen in Ireland (as they have in the EU). This holds true for both sexes. For prime-age workers, inactivity has declined in Ireland and the Netherlands, but has risen slightly in Denmark. The decline results exclusively from a decrease in women's inactivity, while men's inactivity rates have increased in all countries (even in Denmark) during the period. Finally, for older workers, inactivity rates have risen in all countries. Again, while older men's inactivity rates have risen everywhere, women's rates have declined in Ireland and the Netherlands, in line with the trend towards higher labour market participation of women. OECD data for 1995/97 suggest that in Austria, too, youth and older workers' inactivity rates have tended to (moderately) increase and those of prime-age workers to decline (OECD, 1998b).

The most important reason for inactivity of the 15–64 year-olds is retirement, which accounts for around 60 per cent of inactivity in Austria

Table 2.23. Inactivity rates by sex and age, 1983 and 1996[1]

Country	1983			1996		
	Men	Women	Total	Men	Women	Total
			15–24 years			
Austria	n.a.	n.a.	n.a.	37.2	43.6	40.4
Denmark	37.7	43.2	40.3	23.5	29.3	26.3
Ireland	40.9	50.0	45.3	53.4	59.9	56.6
Netherlands	55.6	55.8	55.7	38.8	39.1	38.9
EU	46.5	54.3	50.3	50.3	57.2	53.7
			25–54 years			
Austria	n.a.	n.a.	n.a.	7.1	26.1	16.5
Denmark	5.7	15.9	10.9	7.3	17.9	12.5
Ireland	5.1	63.0	33.4	8.1	42.6	25.4
Netherlands	6.6	56.8	31.2	7.3	32.4	19.6
EU	4.7	43.5	24.2	7.5	30.6	19.0
			55 years and over[2]			
Austria	n.a.	n.a.	n.a.	75.8	92.3	85.4
Denmark	62.2	81.4	72.7	71.5	84.5	78.5
Ireland	52.9	89.1	71.9	61.8	88.7	76.1
Netherlands	70.4	93.4	83.1	76.7	91.4	84.7
EU	66.1	87.8	78.7	73.2	87.9	81.4

n.a. = not available.
Notes: [1] Inactive people of each group as percentage of the population of the same group. [2] The age group "55 years and over" includes not only people aged 55–64, but also those aged 65 and over.
Source: Eurostat: *Labour Force Survey*, various issues.

and Denmark, and 45 per cent in the Netherlands (there are no data for Ireland). Other important reasons are personal or family responsibilities, training and disability. Differences are large between countries, sex and age. In the Netherlands, personal and family responsibilities are the second largest reason for inactivity, and in Austria too such responsibilities account for 15 per cent of the reasons for inactivity. Education and training are important in all three countries, while disability and illness are important in Denmark and the Netherlands, but not in Austria. As an approximation for discouraged workers, the category of those who believe that no work is available is of minor quantitative importance in the three countries.

Women tend to be much less often inactive because of retirement, training and invalidity. Denmark has the most equal gender distribution with regard to all these categories. Except for Denmark, personal and family responsibilities are an important reason for women's inactivity: they are the second most important reason in Austria, and the most important reason (before retirement) in the Netherlands. Although this reason for inactivity also plays a larger role for men in Denmark than in the two other countries, in general family responsibilities are still a very minor reason for male inactivity.

Furthermore, there is a household dimension to inactivity, and for the three countries for which figures are available, the share of inactives living in households with nobody at work varies between 30 per cent in Ireland, 35 per cent in Austria and slightly above 40 per cent in the Netherlands. Contrary to the case of the unemployed, in Ireland and the Netherlands the shares of inactives living in jobless households has tended to increase in the present employment boom. Again, this is linked to age and early retirement or functional equivalents such as invalidity pensions, and also to the high share of inactive prime-age men.

Dependency rates

High employment rates, low unemployment rates and low inactivity rates are signs of societies in which most people participate in economic life, and such a state of affairs matches ILO goals if the jobs provided are also decent.

However, as a marked feature of their Welfare States, all European countries have a large number of recipients in diverse social transfer schemes, which cut across the categories of the employed, the unemployed and the inactives: the most important of these are unemployment insurance and assistance benefits, invalidity benefits, early or regular retirement benefits, and maternity and sickness benefits.

It has often been put forward that countries are successful in curbing open unemployment only because they hide their unemployed in such social transfer schemes. This has been argued, for example, in the case of the Dutch invalidity pension scheme, with about 900,000 benefit recipients. A recent study carried out by the Netherlands Economic Institute (NEI), on behalf of the Dutch Ministry of Social Affairs and Employment, shows that the successful countries do not have more people in these schemes than the countries with high unemployment rates. Dependency rates are defined as the percentage of people living on benefits per employed person (e.g. a ratio of 0.803 means that for each 1,000 employed, 803 live on benefits; maternity and sickness benefits are excluded from the analysis). Table 2.24 shows that while overall European dependency rates (row A) are markedly higher than those in the United States, both Denmark and the Netherlands are among the countries with the lowest rates in Europe. Both countries have also seen a decline in their rates in recent years (see table 2.24; no data available for Ireland). Austria has somewhat higher rates, but still below French, Belgian or British levels.

Table 2.24 (row B) shows the same dependency rates but only for the population of working age, thus excluding a large portion of old-age pensioners. Again, both Denmark and the Netherlands are among the European countries with the lowest values, and the ratio has declined in recent years. The decline was stronger here than for overall dependency rates, showing probably the impact of falling unemployment. Austria, Belgium and France have the highest rates, an effect of early retirement provisions. The United States has

Table 2.24. Social benefit dependency rates[1], various industrialized countries, 1980–96

		Denmark	Netherlands	Belgium	France	United Kingdom	Austria	Sweden	Germany	Japan	United States
A	1980	0.721	0.672	0.800	0.619	0.616	0.770	0.672	0.710	n.a.	0.543
B	1980	0.333	0.318	0.417	0.295	0.265	0.541	0.262	0.315	n.a.	0.255
A	1990	0.768	0.824	1.038	0.808	0.689	0.790	0.722	0.723	0.533	0.507
B	1990	0.383	0.426	0.590	0.441	0.319	0.558	0.280	0.360	0.286	0.215
A	1993	0.845	0.837	1.087	0.898	0.845	0.857	0.969	0.763	0.586	0.546
B	1993	0.438	0.433	0.675	0.500	0.433	0.609	0.433	0.399	0.305	0.240
A	1996	0.803	0.792	1.106	0.926	0.825	0.840	0.913	0.814	0.637	0.520
B	1996	0.402	0.394	0.665	0.502	0.422	0.593	0.401	0.425	0.323	0.220

Notes: A: Benefit recipients per person employed 15 years and older. B: Benefit recipients per person employed 15 to 65 years.
[1] Excluding maternity and sickness.
Source: Netherlands Economic Institute, 1999.

Table 2.25. Potential labour force divided into earned income, social benefits, and no income, full-time equivalents, 1996 (percentages)

Country	Earned income	Social benefits	No income	Total
Austria	57	34	10	100
Belgium	52	35	14	100
Denmark	60	24	15	100
France	52	26	22	100
Germany	55	23	22	100
Netherlands	49	19	32	100
Sweden	54	24	22	100
United Kingdom	57	24	18	100
Japan	68	22	10	100
United States	64	14	22	100

Note: This category differs from the employment rate in full-time equivalents because sickness and maternity are subtracted from earned income and enclosed in the category of social benefits.
Source: Netherlands Economic Institute, 1999.

low rates, corresponding to an economy with low social benefits (but high poverty levels).

Are dependency rates sustainable?

While the employment success cases (except Austria) do not have higher benefit dependency rates than other European countries with more unemployment, benefit dependency rates in Europe are high. They are also bound to increase through the double effects of low fertility and increasing life expectancy (resulting in an ageing workforce). Therefore, some corrections of former supply-reduction policies must be made and employment rates should be increased, in particular for older workers.

However, the social consequences of a significant shift in such policies have to be carefully measured. A policy for more decent jobs being delivered by economic growth should impact favourably on dependency rates. A shift from "passive" to "active" benefits (through the extension of active labour market policy) should also be pursued. Cuts in benefit systems without alternatives might, however, simply lead to an increase in the working poor. In such a case, in-work benefits (benefits granted on the grounds that somebody is working but earns low wages) in different forms are a better alternative. The "European" option would then consist of a consequent policy of lowering wage costs (e.g. by substantial cuts in social security contributions), while increasing net income for low-paid workers. While the American system of a negative income tax (Earned Income Tax Credit) could also be a model for such a policy, the rates at which low wages are subsidized should probably be higher in Europe – at least in high-wage countries – than in the United States.

Another way to analyse the potential labour force (the working-age population 15–64 years old) is to break it down by main source of income.

As table 2.25 shows, both Austria and Denmark are among the European countries with the largest share of people living on earned income. Both countries have at the same time a rather high percentage of people living on social benefits (the share in Austria is particularly high), while the share of the Dutch living on welfare is among the lowest in Europe, as is the percentage of people living on earned income in full-time equivalents (this is also because of high part-time rates). Both in Denmark and Austria, low shares of the potential labour force earn no income at all, while the percentage of this category is high in the Netherlands. This could be due to family patterns (e.g. a large percentage of women and children, as well as spouses of pensioners, are still living in households of the male breadwinner type) and social security principles (e.g. targeting families), but additional research is needed for a thorough explanation.

CONCLUSION

Labour market success is multidimensional and relative. Unemployment has fallen to low levels in Denmark and the Netherlands, has remained at low levels in Austria and has rapidly declined in Ireland, although it is still relatively high there. But it is difficult to rank countries even with such a simple indicator: rank order depends on whether we consider present unemployment levels (in this case, the Netherlands is clearly in the lead), levels over the long term (which would see Austria in front), the magnitude of decline in the unemployment rates in percentage points (which would see Ireland in leading position) or in percentages (which again would place the Netherlands first).

For employment indicators, too, the dimension of the indicator and the time frame chosen (employment rates, employment growth, long term, short term) affect ranking. While Ireland is clearly leading in employment growth over the short term, the longer-term result is less impressive and both the Netherlands and Austria do much better. A ranking of present employment rates, a main indicator for success in European labour markets, would see Denmark on top, followed by Austria. If changes in employment rates were the benchmark, the Netherlands and Ireland would come out top, while Denmark would come last. If full-time equivalent rates were the benchmark, then the Netherlands would be last (and both the Netherlands and Ireland would even fall below the EU average), while Denmark would again be first followed closely by Austria. The question here is: Should only full-time work be considered "decent" work (ILO, 1999), or is part-time work equally "decent"? We think that individual choice is relevant here and that voluntary part-time work, with a reasonable number of working hours, might indeed be considered "decent" work, at least in certain phases of working life.

On a more qualitative level, a prominent indicator for equality of opportunity for men and women is the gender gap. Gender gaps exist in all labour market dimensions, such as employment, unemployment and inactivity, and in their structural components as well. A good indicator to measure the gender gap in employment is the full-time equivalent employment rate, which also takes into account the working-time differentials between men and women. The ranking of this rate shows Denmark most equal, albeit still with a 17-point difference between male and female full-time equivalent employment rates, followed by Austria (27 points) and Ireland (28 points). The Netherlands brings up the rear with a 36-point difference, because of the high share of part-time work among Dutch women.

Of course, one may in principle construct composite ranking indicators. There are different methods of doing this, but all are questionable, as they depend very much on the indicators chosen. The Bertelsmann Foundation uses a seven-variable regression model, while the European Commission uses the method of diamond charts, which allow the graphical presentation of four indicators and the extent of success by measuring the graph's surface. According to the latter method, Austria and Denmark are amongst the three best-performing countries in the Union.[3] (For a presentation and discussion, see Annex II.)

While the above analysis has clearly shown the different dimensions of success and failure in the labour market, the four countries can be classified as successful on at least three grounds. First, they have all succeeded in either bringing unemployment down or maintaining it at low levels. Second, they have either reached, or are on the way to reaching, high employment rates. Third, and this applies at present more to Ireland, the Netherlands and Denmark than to Austria, employment growth has been significant.

However, even these countries still face many problems in their labour markets. First, long-term unemployment, while lower, is still a problem, in particular in the Netherlands and Ireland, and to a smaller extent also in Austria and Denmark. While there will always be a certain amount of joblessness because of frictional and structural unemployment (due to sectoral and technological shifts), long-term unemployment should be reduced to minimum levels.

Second, youth unemployment has been considerably reduced, but it is still high in Ireland and has recently grown again in Austria. Youth gaps should be closed and indeed reversed, as working life should not start with periods of unemployment.

Third, gender gaps should also be closed, although this requires some discussion of the types of household seen as the target: at present several major types of household participation in the labour market are evident. First is the single-earner household for both women and men (a form which is on the increase) or the single "breadwinner" type (here, the "male bread-winner" variant, which was once dominant, is generally on the decline, but is still important in Ireland). In addition, there are different kinds of dual-earner households (either with men and women working full time as in Denmark, and, to a lesser extent, also in Austria, or men working full time and women working part time, as in the Netherlands). Finally, there are the households where no one works. While the latter can be excluded as a target, the dual-earner society, where both men and women work full time, is one in which gender gaps would have to be closed in all dimensions. If the Dutch pattern is the target, gender gaps in part-time work are here to stay. Such societal trends seem to determine the type of labour supply in labour markets.

Education is a strong driving force for higher labour market participation, and family structures also strongly influence labour supply. The challenge for employment systems will be to offer the demand that this supply will need. If there is something approaching a linear development and a convergence in societies, then the Danish model of the dual-earner society will indeed be the model of the future. But different nations, with their specific traditions and cultures, might offer a choice of alternatives for family structures that will influence labour market supply, and we will face a heterogeneity of such structures with differentiated labour supply behaviour. This will go (and already goes) hand in hand with a diversity of working-time patterns. If so, labour demand will have to be very responsive in order to match supply (for these developments see Rubery, forthcoming; Bosch, forthcoming).

Notes

[1] Employment rates measure the number of (self- or dependent) employed as a proportion of the total population of working age. Increases indicate that a greater number of people are holding jobs. However, as the numerator also changes (because of population growth or decline), different population growth rates have different implications for the employment rate: if population increases strongly (as in Ireland, and to some extent also in the Netherlands and Austria), employment has to outgrow population growth if employment rates are to rise. It is (arithmetically at least) easier to maintain high rates or improve them if population is increasing only moderately, as in Denmark.

[2] In this international comparison the arguments are based on figures in ILO labour force terms. National register rates are usually higher than the survey rates, because some of the registered unemployed might not be available for work (e.g. the elderly) or might not have actively searched (discouraged while receiving benefits), and therefore do not fall under the labour force survey definition.

[3] European Commission: *Joint Employment Report*, 1998.

REASONS FOR SUCCESS

3

Having outlined in Chapter 2 the dimensions of relative success, as well as the remaining problems faced by the four countries under review, we now turn to the explanation of success. We highlight the contributions of three policy fields (or institutions) that have had a major influence on developments in labour market macroeconomic policy, social dialogue and labour market policies. The latter two policy fields are linked to what institutional economists consider the most important labour market institutions: wage formation (collective bargaining), unemployment benefit systems, and labour market policy and job security provisions (Gual, 1998). For example, social dialogue/industrial relations is primarily a wage-setting institution, but its agenda is actually wider and includes social security, working time and even gender policies. Also, employment protection is a result of the collective bargaining process in the four countries studied, which all more or less have a system of "corporatist governance", in which the State and the social partners share policy-making powers. In addition to the gender dimension, which concerns practically all policy fields, the following elements will be discussed in particular:

1. *Macroeconomic policy*: monetary and fiscal policies are levers which can be used to influence supply and demand in the labour market. Basic macro-economic relations between, for example, economic growth and its components and investment and employment, are important in order to understand the development of the labour market in the countries under review. This and the following sections on industrial relations and labour market policy also include a partial analysis of social security, employment security and the tax system: all three dimensions are important, as they influence both supply and demand in the labour market and set incentives and disincentives.
2. *Social dialogue and industrial relations*: the reinvigoration of social dialogue marked a starting point for the turnaround in labour markets in the

four countries. Social dialogue exists on many levels, and ranges from information and discussion to the concrete implementation of policies. Active participation of the social partners in the administration of the social security system and the employment service is also included in systems of corporatist governance. All the countries under review practise different systems of "corporatist governance", that is to say that all important reforms in the labour market and in social security legislation are usually the outcome of bargaining between the government and the social partners.

3. *Labour market policy*: we refer here to a concept of labour market policy which includes both income protection (so-called "passive labour market policy") and active labour market policy measures such as labour market training and job creation. The implementing agencies (largely the public employment service) are included in the analysis. Labour market policies are a more direct way of intervening in the labour market than more general macroeconomic policies, and have both supply- and demand-side implications.

In the following sections, the discussion will focus on these three items. However, other important elements of employment systems, such as education and training systems or working-time policies, will also be considered.

MACROECONOMICS AND EMPLOYMENT SUCCESS

This section deals with the contribution of macroeconomic policy to employment success. It seems that, in particular, small economies such as those under review have difficulty in credibly pursuing tough currency and stabilization policies, their currencies being vulnerable to speculation. The decision to peg their currency to the bigger economies (and in particular the Deutschmark, which played a central role within the European Monetary System – EMS), is certainly one of the factors which made the countries credible. From this follows a policy of "tight money", for which the *Bundesbank* (and now the European Central Bank) stands. The *Bundesbank* has been accused at times of worsening unemployment by giving priority to price stability and raising interest rates, as soon as overheating of the economy threatened. In the long term, however, tight monetary policy seems to have paid off. Inflation is nearly everywhere at historically low levels and interest rates are down. The EU countries have also engaged in budget consolidation, a trend which has been reinforced by the Maastricht convergence criteria.

The four small economies under review have a large "degree of openness", as expressed by the ratio of imports and exports to GDP. Their domestic markets being quite small, all the countries are large exporters and importers of goods and services. For them globalization seems to be paying off, as is shown by the present recovery, which has also affected the labour market.

This book does not deal with industrial and technology policy, although this might also have contributed to success. Nor does it deal with product and service market developments, although labour markets depend on the changes and dynamics of these markets. However, the question of the real impact of certain competitive sectors on labour markets, such as the transport cluster in the Netherlands, environmentally friendly energy production in Denmark, the new automobile cluster in Austria or the computer technology sector in Ireland, to name only a few, can be decisive. The financial markets also produce spill-overs onto labour markets, as the Asian crisis has clearly shown.

Nor do we address the issue of whether the four countries have pursued "beggar-thy-neighbour" policies, that is, have improved their position at the cost of other countries through unfair competition and competitive devaluations. We do not think that a country should be accused of unfair competition, when its competitive advantages derive from a de facto devaluation due, for example, to unit labour cost reduction. Such competitive advantages might have helped some countries (the argument has been put forward in the case of the Netherlands), but this seems to be part of the economic game. Other countries might have used capital investments to push up their productivity (in other sectors) and were also able to compete with lower labour costs. Also, tax differentials might have played some role, especially Ireland's low corporate tax rates. Again, loopholes and depreciation mechanisms might have lowered high nominal tax rates in other countries to equally low levels. In general, the economy seems not to be a zero sum game but is rather mutually reinforcing given the close interlinkages in the globalized (or better here "Europeanized") economies. However, the realization of the EMU will certainly increase pressures for the harmonization of tax systems.

Nor do we assess the contribution of the European structural funds, which has been especially substantial in Ireland, where they have contributed to between 2 and 3.5 per cent of GNP (in different years). It seems that this money has reached its objective of bringing the Irish economy nearer the European average GDP, and funds from that source will consequently be phased out (for details, see O'Connell, 1999).

A precondition for employment recovery is economic growth. Despite claims that the advanced economies have moved towards jobless growth, this seems to hold true only for the industrial sector, owing to its labour-saving rationalization potential, but not for the service sector. Because of the shift towards the service sector with its lower productivity, the overall employment intensity of economic growth is usually increasing and not decreasing. Paving the way for higher economic growth and employment is certainly still a major task of macroeconomic policies. Macroeconomic levers for such stimulation are monetary and fiscal policies. After the presentation of some figures on the employment intensity of economic growth, we review these macroeconomic policies in the four countries.

Economic growth and employment intensity

Over the period 1980–96, GDP growth was rather similar in Austria, Denmark and the Netherlands at about 40 per cent (Austria, 40.8 per cent; Denmark, 38.5 per cent; the Netherlands, 42.2 per cent). Ireland's economy grew at an exceptional pace and increased by 106 per cent in the same period.

In annual averages, over the same period the Austrian and Netherlands economies grew by 2.2 per cent, the Danish economy by 2 per cent, and the Irish economy by 4.2 per cent. However, growth patterns became more diversified in recent years and average annual growth rates of GDP over the period 1994–97 are 2.1 per cent in Austria, 2.7 per cent in Denmark, 3.0 per cent in the Netherlands and 9.9 per cent in Ireland. While diversity in economic growth has lately increased, employment performance has been even more varied.

Table 3.1 shows that over this recent period Austria actually lost employment (as did Germany), while increases in employment were strongest in Ireland, followed by the Netherlands and Denmark. The Netherlands and Ireland had even stronger employment growth rates than the United States during the four-year period.

As can be seen from table 3.1, countries have different patterns of economic growth. For example, while the Austrian economy has growth rates similar to the EU average, employment actually declined during the most recent period. As a result, recent Austrian economic growth has been due to higher productivity and not additional jobs (similar to Germany), while the Dutch economy has grown through jobs, and growth is consequently associated with lower productivity growth (similar to the American economy).

Table 3.1. GDP, GDP per employed and per hour worked, employment, population of working age[1] and average hours worked: Average annual growth rates, 1994–97

Country	GDP	GDP/ employed	GDP/hours worked	Employ- ment	Population	Working time	Employment intensity[2]
Austria	2.1	2.3	2.3	−0.2	0.0	0.0	0
Denmark	2.7	1.0	1.9	1.7	0.2	−0.8	0.70
Ireland	9.9	5.3	6.2	4.4	1.6	−0.8	0.62
Netherlands	3.0	0.7	0.8	2.2	0.3	−0.1	0.73
Germany	1.8	2.8	3.1	−1.0	0.0	−0.3	0
France	2.0	1.6	2.3	0.4	0.3	−0.6	0.2
United Kingdom	2.9	1.6	1.7	1.2	0.2	−0.1	0.4
EU	2.3	1.7	2.2	0.5	0.4	−0.3	0.2
United States	3.3	n.a.	n.a.	1.9	0.8	1.1	0.6

Notes: [1]Aged 15–64. [2]Employment divided by economic growth. It shows in a simplistic way how much employment was created for every percentage point of economic growth.

Sources: EU countries: European Commission: *Employment in Europe*, 1998; for the United States: ILO, KILM database; OECD: *Economic Outlook*, Dec. 1998, and *Employment Outlook*, 1998; author's calculations.

Table 3.2. Employment intensity of economic growth, 1985–95 (average annual growth rates)

Country	GDP growth	Employment growth	Employment/GDP
Austria	2.6	0.7	0.27
Denmark	1.7	0.1	0.06
France	2.1	0.3	0.14
Germany	1.4	0.5	0.35
Ireland	5.0	1.5	0.30
Netherlands	2.6	1.8	0.70
United Kingdom	2.3	0.6	0.26
EU 15	2.0	0.4	0.20
United States	2.4	1.5	0.62

Source: OECD: *Employment Outlook*, 1998.

Ireland has both high productivity and employment growth, and Denmark also shows both productivity increases (as expressed by GDP per hour worked) and considerable employment growth. In the latter two countries, productivity per hour has also increased as a consequence of a reduction in average working time.

However, the period of four years may be too short to make out a trend, and we cannot be certain that this pattern will be sustained over the long term. Compared to the longer-term trend, the employment intensity of economic growth has lately risen substantially in three of the four countries reviewed, as can be seen by a comparison between table 3.2 and table 3.1. It appears that since the 1980s Austria has consistently had a low intensity of economic growth, but above the European average, while the Netherlands has had much higher intensities over the long term. Denmark's improvement from a low to high intensity of economic growth is remarkable, and so are the high intensities in Ireland.

Whether or not the recent increases will prove to be sustainable remains to be seen, but it seems that some countries have changed their growth regime from high productivity growth and low employment creation to a more employment-intensive growth pattern. Data on the different employment intensities of growth in different sectors would show that these changes are partly due to sectoral shifts: employment growth is almost exclusively occurring in the lower-productivity service sector, while the industrial sector is usually shedding jobs (an exception is Ireland, where the industrial sector also shows employment increases). For example, Hartog (1999) shows that the highly productive Dutch manufacturing export sector has experienced job losses despite high growth rates. Given overall increasing intensities, this highlights the fact that the employment intensity of economic growth is particularly high in the labour-intensive service sector, and low in manufacturing (see also Schettkat, forthcoming). Working time also plays a role here, and considering total labour volume would, for example, relativize the high Dutch intensity figure. However, as further employment growth will be concentrated in the much less productivity-intensive service sector, this will result in higher employment intensity of economic growth. Higher employment intensity will also reduce the employment threshold, that is, the economic growth rate needed to trigger employment growth.

Schettkat (forthcoming) shows that the relation between economic growth and unemployment (usually represented by Okun's law) has improved especially in Ireland and Denmark, and the impact of growth on unemployment rates in the period 1990–98 is higher in Denmark, Ireland and the Netherlands than in the United States. Austria has always had a weak relation between growth and unemployment, which is, among other factors, due to the high sensitivity of labour supply to the business cycle (see Pichelmann, with Hofer, 1999).

Macroeconomic policy

The usual macroeconomic levers which governments can use to influence the level of economic activity are monetary and fiscal policies. However, wage policy is also a crucial part of macroeconomic policy. But wage formation is central to the systems of "corporatist governance" in which the social partners play a leading role and is therefore not per se a macroeconomic instrument in the hand of governments, although government intervention in wage formation has been frequent (see Visser, forthcoming). Therefore, the wage issue will be addressed in the section on social dialogue and industrial relations, below. These policies must also be coordinated: for example, a tight monetary policy can hardly be compatible with a loose fiscal policy, and it also requires wage restraint in order to succeed in curbing inflation. Although we do not explicitly analyse the issue, coordination seems to be rather efficient in all four countries, since wage policy has come into line with the other elements of macroeconomic policy.

After a period of stagflation (parallel increase of inflation and unemployment) in the late 1970s and early 1980s, Keynesian policies of demand stimulation through expansionary fiscal (and monetary) policies were believed to have become ineffective. In fact, they are today believed to have contributed to the problems of the early 1980s (see, for example, Hartog, 1999). The main criticism of expansionary monetary and fiscal policies was that they had led to higher inflation and higher government debts without producing benefits for the economy. For example, it was argued that high government borrowing requirements had crowded out private capital. Concerning unemployment, the concept of the natural rate of unemployment (or the later NAIRU – non-accelerating-inflation rate of unemployment) suggested that there was only one equilibrium rate of unemployment to which it would inevitably return despite fiscal expansion, which would in the end result only in higher inflation. In other words, there was no trade-off (at least in the long term) between unemployment and inflation as illustrated by the Philips curve. Thus demand policies were seen as ineffective. Instead supply behaviour in labour markets had to be changed in order to reduce unemployment. Published back in 1968 by Milton Friedman and Edmund Phelps in two independent papers, the concept of the natural equilibrium rate of unemployment became a mainstream idea during the late 1980s and 1990s.

Restrictive monetary and fiscal policies, as well as supply-side reforms of the labour market, were seen as the answer. This went together with a change of focus on microeconomic rather than macroeconomic policy-making. For example, the supply side of wages (the cost of labour to firms), rather than their demand side (purchasing power for the economy), was stressed. A tight monetary policy and restrictive government finances were said to result in low inflation and low interest rates, which would in turn stimulate economic activity and employment, and help reduce unemployment. The belief that government debt and intervention crowded out private activities, especially investment, was strong during these years, and even today is a powerful argument for "small" government. Changes in the supply side of the labour market, basically downward flexible wages, and the removal of wage floors set by minimum wages or high social benefits in case of unemployment, were also proposed.

"Rational expectations", based on an argument developed by Lucas (1976), implied that human beings learn from past experience and integrate experience in their choices (Schettkat, forthcoming). This offered an additional argument to those backing tight government policies: as these policies are expected to result in low inflation and low interest rates, investment decisions, for example, would be facilitated.

Given that supply-side arguments became dominant in the 1980s and 1990s (as illustrated by "Reaganomics" and "Thatcherism"), the decisive question in our context is whether such policies have contributed to the success of the four countries. Of course, this synthesis review cannot address this question exhaustively. However, some empirical arguments can be put forward which cast doubt on the validity of certain of these supply-side arguments, while confirming others.

Tight monetary policy

Today nobody would deny that in general tight monetary policy (a policy based more on changing central bank rates than controlling the money supply) is at least partially responsible for low inflation and low interest rates, and has had a beneficial effect on the moderate wage policy pursued by the social partners. But the monetary policy in the countries under review is usually not "home-made": two countries (the Netherlands and

Austria) have pegged their currency to the Deutschmark, and have thus followed the tight monetary policy of the *Bundesbank*. Denmark and Ireland are also indirectly linked to the monetary policy of the *Bundesbank* through the EMS. Such a monetary regime will be continued, and indeed intensified under the EMU, of which three of the countries are full members, while the fourth (Denmark) is a "virtual" member, but in practice copies the monetary policies of the EMU member countries. All countries are therefore by obligation (or in anticipation) under the regime of the Maastricht convergence criteria, perpetuated during the EMU by the Stability and Growth Pact aimed at low inflation, low government deficits and debt ratios, and low interest rates.

At times the *Bundesbank* has been accused of worsening problems by sticking to its tight policy, and it might be that in business cycles the built-in stabilizers are not sufficient and should be bolstered by macroeconomic policy, including temporary periods of "loose" monetary and fiscal policy. However, this should happen within tight margins and must be exactly timed (which is difficult, as macroeconomic steering of the economy is more of an art than a science).

The small countries under review have all more or less renounced an autonomous monetary policy and have followed the stability-oriented policy of the *Bundesbank*. A tight monetary policy, aimed at price stability, needs a wage policy which accommodates it. It is one of the achievements of "corporatist governance" that such a wage policy, oriented towards macroeconomic stability, has been one factor behind the recovery of labour markets.

Fiscal policy

While monetary policy can more or less be treated as exogenous, did fiscal policy play any role in the present upswing? Because of the construction of the EMU, all countries have been subject to a policy of consolidating their government finances. Table 3.3 shows this convincingly: all four countries meet or surpass the Maastricht criterion on budget deficits (3 per cent of GDP); government debt is still somewhat higher than the 60 per cent of GDP target, but (except for Austria) is declining as well.

However, while Maastricht has led to a reduction in government spending, fiscal policy has still been used to stimulate economic activity and labour markets during the 1990s, although in a more limited range than in the 1970s and early 1980s. For example, in the recession of the early 1990s, a fiscal stimulus (increased government spending and a tax cut) was used to get the Danish economy back to a more sustained growth path. But Austria and Ireland too, and even the Netherlands (to a more limited extent), permitted government deficits to widen during the crisis. There seems to be still some anti-cyclical elements in government spending, even if this has become limited (see table 3.3). Restricted room for manoeuvre is also a

Table 3.3. Fiscal policy, budget consolidation, 1970–98

Year	Government borrowing as % of GDP				Government debt as % of GDP			
	Austria	Denmark	Ireland	Netherlands	Austria	Denmark	Ireland	Netherlands
1970	0.2	0.9	−1.4	0.0	19.4	n.a.	n.a.	51.5
1971	−0.2	0.6	−1.1	0.0	18.2	n.a.	n.a.	49.1
1972	−0.5	0.6	−0.5	0.0	17.5	n.a.	n.a.	46.0
1973	1.2	0.6	0.8	0.0	17.5	n.a.	n.a.	42.8
1974	−1.3	0.3	0.0	0.0	17.6	n.a.	56.5	40.8
1975	−5.6	−2.4	−2.2	0.0	23.9	n.a.	62.4	41.8
1976	−3.4	−0.7	−2.0	0.0	27.4	n.a.	66.9	41.4
1977	−2.4	−0.8	−0.8	−7.3	30.1	n.a.	63.9	40.8
1978	−2.4	−2.1	−2.3	−9.4	33.9	n.a.	65.9	42.1
1979	−2.6	−0.8	−3.0	−11.1	36.0	n.a.	71.2	44.1
1980	−2.9	0.0	−4.2	−12.3	37.3	44.7	72.7	46.9
1981	−3.7	−1.9	−5.4	−13.0	39.3	54.9	77.4	50.9
1982	−3.3	−2.8	−6.6	−13.4	41.8	67.0	83.3	56.5
1983	−2.6	−3.2	−5.8	−11.4	46.5	77.8	97.3	62.7
1984	−1.9	−2.8	−5.5	−9.5	48.6	79.3	101.6	67.0
1985	−1.2	−2.9	−3.6	−10.9	50.5	76.6	104.6	71.7
1986	−1.3	−2.7	−5.1	−10.7	54.9	73.4	116.3	73.5
1987	−1.9	−1.9	−5.9	−8.6	58.7	70.2	117.6	76.2
1988	−2.2	−1.7	−4.6	−4.5	59.5	68.2	113.6	79.2
1989	0.1	−1.2	−4.7	−1.8	58.9	66.9	103.7	79.1
1990	−2.1	−1.6	−5.1	−2.3	58.3	68.0	96.3	78.8
1991	−3.3	−2.0	−2.9	−2.4	58.7	69.1	96.6	78.8
1992	−2.8	−3.8	−3.9	−2.5	58.3	73.2	94.0	79.6
1993	−3.5	−5.6	−3.2	−2.5	62.8	82.6	97.1	80.6
1994	−2.4	−5.6	−3.4	−1.8	65.1	80.5	91.0	77.3
1995	−3.6	−5.0	−4.1	−2.1	69.3	76.9	84.9	79.5
1996	−3.8	−4.2	−2.4	−0.9	69.8	74.8	76.5	78.5
1997	−3.2	−3.2	−2.3	−1.2	71.3	71.5	72.0	74.5
1998	−2.7	−3.0	−1.7	−1.0	72.6	66.5	67.3	72.6

Sources: Schettkat (forthcoming). Computations based on OECD statistics: *Economic Outlook*, OECD CD-ROM.

consequence of the increasing importance of structural components of government expenditure (e.g. statutory benefits and interest payments).

GDP expenditure components

Expressed as a percentage of GDP, government expenditure is clearly declining in all four countries. The fall is most accentuated in Ireland and the Netherlands, and is more moderate in Austria and Denmark. With 58.2 per cent of GDP, Denmark still had the highest level of government expenditure in 1997, followed by Austria with 51.8 per cent and the Netherlands with around 50 per cent. Ireland has reduced its government spending in relation to GDP from almost 50 per cent in the period 1979–89 to 35 per cent in 1997. This is also a consequence of high economic growth (table 3.4).

However, such shares give a skewed picture of real government expenditure. If we look at GDP expenditure aggregates, we see several shifts occurring: the share of public consumption expenditure is generally declining, most dramatically in Ireland. But domestic demand as a whole is also declining, and net exports account for much more prominent shares (table 3.4).

Ireland and the Netherlands in particular are experiencing strong net export growth and these two economies are growing increasingly by virtue of their real export increases. This is confirmed not only by a growing share of exports within GDP, but also absolute export growth, expressed in 1990 prices in national currency (table 3.5). However, table 3.5 also shows another feature of growth in the four countries: while government consumption has declined as *a share* of GDP, it has increased in all countries since 1990 *in absolute real figures*, and especially strongly in Ireland.

As can be seen from table 3.5, government consumption is still important for growth, even if it has declined as a share. Private consumption is the most essential element of GDP growth in all countries, and fixed capital formation (a part of which is also public) is the second most important category (expressed as a share of GDP) in three countries. Only in Denmark have public consumption expenditure increases been more important than increases in capital formation, reflecting the large government sector in this country. The share of government consumption in total domestic demand in 1996 was 18 per cent in Austria, 26 per cent in Denmark, and 15 per cent in both Ireland and the Netherlands.

The points made above lead to the conclusion that even though government expenditure is on the decline, it is still a factor for growth. It does not seem to crowd out private consumption or investment, as Schettkat (forthcoming) notes. The least one can say is that there is no zero-sum game between government and private expenditure: the figures show much more the idea of mutual support, with public consumption stimulating private consumption and also having beneficial effects for capital formation (Schettkat, forthcoming). In addition, the figures indicate some room for manoeuvre for public demand policies, at least in the short term as in Denmark. According to our data, correlations between government consumption expenditure and consumer price development are for all four countries consistently and significantly negative: this seems to suggest that inflation is rather independent of government spending. In fact, inflation has fallen to very low levels today (partly because of falling prices on world markets, e.g. energy) and seems not to present a significant danger. Some experts even fear deflationary trends which could start the economy on a downward spiral.

A point which can be made here is that (temporary) expansionary policies seem not to lead to persistent inflation, although this certainly depends on their magnitude. Furthermore, government consumption appears to support the economy and does not crowd out private initiative, at least not in any

Table 3.4 GDP expenditure aggregates 1980–96[1] (% of real GDP)

Main aggregates	Austria				Denmark				Ireland				Netherlands			
	1980	1985	1990	1996	1980	1985	1990	1996	1980	1985	1990	1996	1980	1985	1990	1996
Public consumption expenditure	20.3	20.6	18.6	18.3	27.9	26.4	25.3	24.3	20.9	19.3	14.8	12.2	14.7	15.2	14.5	13.6
Private consumption expenditure	55.0	55.9	55.9	57.0	56.0	54.2	51.9	54.0	68.5	61.5	58.1	51.4	62.6	59.6	58.7	58.6
Gross fixed capital formation	22.9	21.0	23.3	24.5	18.2	17.9	17.4	16.0	24.7	18.8	18.8	16.1	21.5	20.3	20.9	20.4
Increase in stocks	4.0	2.0	0.9	0.6	−0.4	0.8	−0.1	0.6	−0.6	1.2	2.4	0.9	1.5	0.7	1.3	0.2
Total domestic demand	102.1	99.6	98.7	100.4	101.7	99.4	94.6	94.8	113.5	100.7	94.1	80.5	100.3	95.8	95.4	92.7
Exports of goods and services	30.0	35.3	40.2	46.8	27.2	30.2	35.5	38.8	37.1	48.3	58.7	80.0	44.0	48.7	54.2	61.7
Imports of goods and services	31.8	34.6	38.9	47.0	27.7	28.8	30.1	33.5	45.9	47.4	52.8	60.5	43.8	44.7	49.5	54.2
Net exports of goods and services	−1.7	0.7	1.3	−0.2	−0.5	1.4	5.4	5.3	−8.9	0.9	5.9	19.5	0.2	3.9	4.6	7.5
Real GDP – total	100.0	100.0	100.0	100.0	100.0	100.0	100.0	100.0	100.0	100.0	100.0	100.0	100.0	100.0	100.0	100.0

Note: [1]At 1990 prices.
Source: OECD: *National Accounts*, 1960–96.

Table 3.5. Real GDP by expenditure components: Growth rates, 1990–96
(percentages)

	Austria	Denmark	Ireland	Netherlands
GDP	11.40	12.50	38.10	13.90
Public consumption	9.50	8.20	17.40	7.07
Private consumption	13.50	16.80	25.10	13.60
Gross fixed capital formation	17.10	5.20	23.60	11.30
Total domestic demand	13.30	13.40	21.90	11.10
Exports of goods and services	27.70	22.10	72.40	27.50

Sources: CEPR data bank; ILO on basis of OECD: *National Accounts*, 1960–96.

dramatic way. With quasi-fixed exchange rates through the pegging of curren-cies to the Deutschmark (and the Euro), no effect on exchange relations is to be feared either. However, for open economies, a certain percentage of any demand expansion will result in increased imports and thus dampen the effects on the national economy. Whether longer-term fiscal expansion would also be non-inflationary remains to be seen. In any case, given the Maastricht criteria, there is no danger that countries will revert to such a policy to any significant extent. Within the margin given (for the time being 3 per cent), countries should, however, use their room for manoeuvre if the need arises, without fear of inflationary pressures.

Government (and social security) revenue

During the heyday of supply-side economics, the revenue side of government (e.g. taxes and social contributions) was much debated. For example, the "Laffer curve" suggested that "more can be less" in taxation; in other words, a reduction in tax rates will ultimately result in higher revenues for the State, as high taxes deter economic activity and lead also to tax evasion. In particular, corporate tax was targeted for reduction, as it is linked to investment and employment creation. Also the tax wedge (the gap between gross and after-tax pay) was said to hinder both labour demand and labour supply. In particu-lar, marginal wedges and marginal tax rates were said to set wrong incentives. For example, if for each gross money unit earned one gets only a small fraction in additional net pay, there is no strong incentive to work more hours. On the other hand, for the unemployed or the poor who live on benefits, the additional income from work is low, with high marginal tax rates. Thus unemployment and/or poverty traps might develop. Finally, labour taxes (social insurance con-tributions) were accused of impacting negatively on employment, especially on low-skilled, low-wage employment.

Several policy proposals followed from these propositions, some of which were also implemented (not all can be mentioned here). For example, the *White Paper on growth, competitiveness and employment* by the European

Commission (1993) advocated a reduction in employers' social security contributions, especially for the low end of the wage distribution, totalling about 2 per cent of GDP. Such a reduction of social security contributions for the low skilled has, for example, recently been implemented in the Netherlands, where since 1996 employers have qualified for a subsidy in the form of a labour tax reduction for their low-wage workers (around 800,000 subsidized persons in 1996).

In order to redress the disincentive to take up work and free people from the unemployment trap, several proposals were put forward: in-work benefits, that is to say, benefits which are paid only on the condition of being employed or taking up a job. In Ireland, family income supplements and a "back-to-work" allowance are designed to cope with such disincentives. The back-to-work allowance permits social benefits to be retained for three years (during which they are progressively reduced), while working as an employee or as self-employed. Another way to cope with the problem is the reduction of the marginal tax rate for low-wage employees; this was done for example in Austria, but also in the 1994 Danish tax reform.

In Austria corporate taxes have also been lowered. Ireland has the lowest corporate tax rates for foreign investors (10 per cent), and this rate seems to be one of the reasons why so much inward investment flows to Ireland (see below). As corporate tax regimes are distorting competitiveness, there is much discussion about their harmonization within the EU.

Table 3.6 shows the different profiles of tax revenue in the four countries: income and profits are the main tax source in Denmark, whereas social contributions provide only a small share of revenue. In Ireland, too, social contributions are not a major revenue source; they are most important in Austria and the Netherlands. In Ireland, indirect taxes (VAT) and income taxes are of equal importance. In Denmark, there has recently been a marginal shift towards "green taxes" (Walter, 1999).

Whereas in Austria and Ireland, as in the EU in general, employers pay a

Table 3.6. Main sources of government revenue as a percentage of total revenue, 1996

Country	Income and profits	Social security	Payroll	Property	Goods and services	Other	
Austria	26.7	36.2	6.7	1.5	27.7	1.2	100
Denmark	60.3	3.1	0.5	3.5	32.4	0.2	100
Ireland	39.1	14.4	1.2	4.5	40.7	n.a.	100
Netherlands	26.4	41.8	n.a.	4.0	27.4	0.5	100
EU 15	33.9	29.4	0.9	4.2	31.0	0.5	100

n.a. = not available.
Source: Walter, 1999.

Table 3.7. Average tax wedge, 1996[1]

Family-type	Single, no children	Single, no children	Single, no children	Single, 2 children	Married, 2 children	Married, 2 children	Married, 2 children	Married, no children
Wage level (% of APW[2])	67	100	167	67	100–0	100–33[3]	100–67[3]	100–33[3]
Austria	37.4	41.5	45.8	16.3	28.0	30.2	32.6	39.4
Denmark	41.3	44.8	52.6	13.6	31.1	36.5	39.5	41.3
Ireland	26.5	36.1	45.7	2.6	25.6	26.5	28.7	29.7
Netherlands	39.3	43.8	44.2	22.3	33.5	35.9	38.1	40.7

Notes: [1] Employees' and employers' social security contributions and personal income tax less transfer payments as a percentage of gross labour costs, by family type and wage level. [2] Average production worker. [3] Two-earner family.

Source: Walter, 1999.

larger share of social contributions than employees, in Denmark and also in the Netherlands, the employees pay more; their share of total social contributions is around 76 per cent in the Netherlands and 80 per cent in Denmark. This partly reflects a fall in employers' share in the early 1990s.

The average tax wedge is shown in table 3.7. It depends on family and income status and is highest for single people earning above-average production worker wages and lowest for single-earner families with two children. The tax wedge is somewhat higher in Denmark and the Netherlands than in Austria and Ireland (see Walter, p. 33). Marginal tax rates are even higher, and are less dependent on family and income status.

These differences show that tax harmonization has a long way to go in the EU and that policy proposals have to be fine-tuned to the specific tax profile of the country concerned. Nevertheless, some common trends in tax policies have emerged: taxes on labour have been trimmed down, and marginal tax rates and social security contributions have been lowered, especially for the low-wage sector (with the exception of Denmark, which has exceptionally low, but increasing social contributions); top income tax rates have also been lowered; at the same time, however, the tax base pwas broadened to include some fringe benefits and even some transfer payments; individual taxation is on the increase and the tax structure has been simplified (see Walter, 1998; OECD, 1995b).

Table 3.8 shows that as a percentage share of GDP, total current receipts have declined in Ireland and the Netherlands, matching the decrease in the expenditure share. They have even grown moderately in Austria and Denmark, both countries with a large share of public sector jobs. This growth occurred also in the EU as a whole. Again, the decline in shares hides an absolute real increase in tax revenues in all countries.

Table 3.8. General government financial balances: A comparison between four EU countries and the EU, 1979–97 (as percentage of GDP at market prices)

	Austria				Denmark				Ireland				Netherlands				European Union[1]			
	1979-89	1990-95	1996	1997	1979-89	1990-95	1996	1997	1979-89	1990-95	1996	1997	1979-89	1990-95	1996	1997	1979-89	1990-95	1996	1997
Total current receipts	47.8	48.1	48.2	48.6	54.6	57.3	58.8	58.1	38.6	37.4	34.8	34.4	53.1	51.2	48.3	47.7	44.2	45.6	46.3	46.4
Total direct taxes	13.5	13.9	14.5	15.2	27.7	30.5	31.9	31.3	13.3	14.4	14.0	14.1	14.2	15.3	12.8	12.0	12.6	12.9	12.8	13.0
Total indirect taxes	16.5	15.7	14.9	14.8	18.6	17.7	18.3	18.4	16.9	15.5	14.7	14.4	12.4	12.7	13.1	13.2	13.4	13.6	14.0	14.1
Social security contributions	14.9	15.4	15.7	15.7	2.5	2.7	2.8	2.8	5.1	5.2	4.5	4.4	19.7	18.5	18.6	19.1	14.6	15.6	16.1	15.9
Other current receipts	3.0	3.1	3.1	2.9	5.8	6.4	5.8	5.6	3.4	2.3	1.6	1.5	6.9	4.7	3.8	3.4	3.7	3.6	3.4	3.4
Total current expenditure	45.0	46.9	47.4	46.9	54.0	57.9	58.0	55.8	43.7	38.1	34.5	33.2	53.3	52.0	48.6	47.2	44.3	47.0	47.6	46.6
Government consumption, of which:	18.6	18.5	18.6	18.2	26.1	25.6	25.2	24.8	17.4	15.4	14.3	14.0	16.4	14.5	14.1	13.9	19.0	19.1	18.9	18.5
Compensation of employees	12.5	12.5	12.5	12.2	18.6	18.3	18.0	17.8	12.2	10.6	9.7	9.6	11.8	9.9	9.5	9.3	12.5	12.1	11.6	11.4
Actual interest payments	3.3	4.2	4.5	4.6	7.2	7.2	6.4	5.9	8.1	6.6	4.5	4.2	5.5	6.1	5.6	5.4	4.2	5.2	5.4	5.3
Total current transfers paid, of which:	23.2	24.2	24.3	24.1	20.8	25.1	26.4	25.1	18.2	16.2	15.7	15.0	31.4	31.3	28.9	27.9	21.1	22.7	23.3	22.8
Enterprises	3.0	3.0	2.3	2.2	3.2	3.8	3.5	3.1	6.8	5.0	4.1	3.9	3.5	2.9	1.9	1.7	2.7	2.3	2.2	2.0
Households	20.0	20.9	21.7	21.4	17.0	20.3	21.6	20.5	14.6	14.5	13.6	13.1	27.4	27.3	25.6	24.8	17.4	19.0	19.8	19.6
Rest of the world (net)	0.2	0.3	0.3	0.5	0.5	1.0	1.3	1.5	-3.2	-3.3	-2.0	-2.0	0.5	1.2	1.4	1.4	0.7	0.9	0.8	0.8
Final capital expenditure	3.9	3.2	3.1	3.1	2.4	1.8	1.7	1.9	3.9	2.2	2.3	2.3	2.6	2.1	2.1	2.2	2.9	2.8	2.4	2.3
Net capital transfers paid	1.8	1.6	1.9	1.8	0.7	0.3	0.5	0.5	0.5	-0.6	-0.4	-0.4	2.3	1.0	0.3	0.7	1.0	0.9	0.6	0.5
Total expenditure	50.7	51.7	52.4	51.8	57.1	59.9	60.2	58.2	48.1	39.6	36.4	35.1	58.1	55.0	51.0	50.1	48.2	50.6	50.6	49.4
Net lending (+) or borrowing (−)	-2.9	-3.5	-4.3	-3.0	-2.6	-2.6	-1.4	-0.3	-9.5	-2.2	-1.6	-0.9	-4.9	-3.8	-2.6	-2.5	-4.0	-4.9	-4.4	-3.0
Net lending (+) or borrowing (−) excluding interest payments	+0.4	+0.7	+0.3	+1.6	+4.6	+4.6	+5.0	+5.6	-1.4	+4.3	+2.9	+3.3	+0.5	+2.3	+3.0	+2.9	+0.2	+0.2	+1.1	+2.2

Note: [1] Data refer to EU 15, Luxembourg excluded; from 1991, data also include the new German Länder.

Source: European Commission: *European Economy Annual Report*, 1997.

Exports stimulate growth

Recent economic growth seems to have been disproportionally driven by a booming export sector. Expressed in real growth rates, exports have risen everywhere more strongly than all other GDP components. The outstanding example is Ireland, where domestic demand now accounts for only 80 per cent of GDP and net exports for the remaining 20 per cent. But exports take a large share in GDP everywhere. In Ireland, real GDP expenditure on exports of goods and services was in 1996 equal to total domestic demand. It corresponds to 67 per cent of domestic demand in the Netherlands, 41 per cent in Denmark and 47 per cent in Austria. The countries differ, however, in their current account balances: for example, in the Netherlands net exports account for a large and growing share of output, while Austria, for example, has recently experienced deficits.

As both Ireland and the Netherlands have recently been the fastest-growing economies in terms of both GDP and jobs, the booming export sector should be one of the causes of both successes. Contrasting pictures emerge, however, in the countries: while Ireland has profited both in growth and jobs from the establishment of export-oriented industries (O'Connell, 1999), Hartog (1999) reports from the Netherlands that growth in the export sector has led to job losses, given the labour displacement effect of its high productivity. More recently, in the wake of a downturn in foreign demand linked to the financial crisis in Asia and Eastern Europe, domestic demand seems to have taken over in some countries "as a locomotive of continued economic growth" (European Commission, 1998f, p. 7).

Foreign direct investment

Foreign direct investment (FDI) is in part related to the export industry. In Ireland, for example, around 45 per cent of the workforce in manufacturing are employed in foreign-owned companies (O'Connell, 1999).

FDI has become more important in all four countries. Increases have been particularly strong in Ireland (where FDI has grown sevenfold), and in Denmark and Austria. The rise has been more moderate in the Netherlands as a percentage of the starting level, although this level is the highest of the four countries. The Netherlands alone attracts more FDI than the three other countries together, around 8 per cent of all European FDI (which puts it fourth in Europe after France, the United Kingdom and Belgium/Luxembourg). In terms of per capita of the labour force, however, Ireland and the Netherlands have the same amount of FDI. While FDI figures include real investment, as well as the product of mergers and acquisitions (the former being probably more important for Ireland), the figures show the importance of FDI for the small open economies. Only Austria is an exception, but it has lately attracted an increasing share of FDI (around 4 per cent of all European Union FDI in 1996). For Ireland in particular, FDI has been a driving force for both economic and employment growth.

Table 3.9. Foreign direct investment inflows, 1985–96 (US$ million)

Country	1985–90	1990–96	Per person in labour force[1]	% of EU FDI[2]
Austria	407	1 340	0.35	1.50
Denmark	514	2 366	0.84	2.60
Ireland	192	1 386	0.92	1.60
Netherlands	5 558	6 903	0.92	8.00
EU	52 685	87 716	0.52	1.00

Notes: [1] 1990–96. [2] 1996.
Sources: *Financial Times*, 2 Nov 1998, p. 11, on the basis of United Nations statistics; author's calculations.

In general, investment is one of the sources of job growth. However, our own calculations do not show a consistent pattern. Investment (gross fixed capital formation) and employment correlate highly in Denmark and Ireland (R^2 of 0.74 and 0.63, respectively), but weakly in the Netherlands and not at all in Austria. Allowing for a lag of one year decreases correlation coefficients for both Denmark and Ireland (R^2 now of 0.63 for Denmark and 0.36 for Ireland), but increases those of the Netherlands (0.7) and also Austria, where it remains, however, weak.

Conclusion

The macroeconomic environment in Europe in general is today much healthier than in the 1970s and 1980s: low inflation, low interest rates, moderate wage growth and consolidated government budgets have restored confidence in the economies. It seems to be accepted that tight monetary policies have helped to create this environment, as has moderate wage growth (see "Social dialogue and employment", below). Economic growth has been driven by foreign and domestic demand, the share of the former tending to increase over the 1990s, but the latter seems to have staged a comeback as foreign demand weakens in the wake of the Asian crisis. Also, domestic and foreign investments have boosted growth and employment. Last but not least, government consumption and investment are part of this favourable situation. Despite claims that government expenses tend to crowd out private demand and investment, it rather seems that the expenditure elements of GDP are mutually supportive. While structural elements of the budget have become more important, in some countries (e.g. Denmark) government expenditure has been used in a targeted and short-term manner, and has supported upswings without creating inflationary pressures.

In addition, the employment intensity of growth has increased, but varies widely across countries, linked also to working-time policies. At least two of the countries experienced a de facto devaluation (through moderate wage policies) against some of their major (European) trade partners, and this has also spurred their economies. However, claims that "beggar-thy-neighbour" policies are the major factors behind superior economic performance seem exaggerated.

Tax policies have been changed, resulting lately in a reduction of social security contributions for the low wage sector and (in some countries) a decrease in the highest rates in the tax progression. Corporate taxes have also been lowered and might have stimulated investments. Tax revenues have risen in absolute figures, but have declined as a share of GDP in Ireland and the Netherlands. In Denmark and Austria, however, increased revenue has also been used to create additional public jobs and has not hindered Denmark from triggering off a general improvement of its economy and the labour market. However, there are still many differences in tax structures and they might distort competition in Europe. Realization of the EMU will in future increase pressure for the harmonization not only of monetary, fiscal and wage policies, but also of tax policies.

SOCIAL DIALOGUE AND EMPLOYMENT

The social dialogue between government, and workers' and employers' organizations can be seen as a crucial factor for the relative labour market success of the countries under review. In this section, the industrial relations systems, of which social dialogue is part, is described and some recent changes in the systems are discussed.

Social dialogue, social partnership and industrial relations

Social dialogue is at the core of the institutions of social partnership in particular, and of industrial relations in general: dialogue is the fuel, while the institutions are the motor, and both are important for progress. In other words, social partnership without a dialogue is condemned to a standstill. Dialogue is conducted on many levels and has different degrees: from the national level to the local level, and from exchange of information and consultation to co-determination, and bargaining and contracting. In addition, social dialogue extends to the administration of certain elements of the social security system and/or the employment service, run by the social partners. However, a distinction should be made between social concertation (social dialogue at the highest level, in which information is exchanged and at which a common view of the state of affairs might be developed), and bargaining over costs and benefits, which is the distributional aspect of the dialogue.

Different names have been given to these governance systems, which in addition to the government give a large role to the social partners in policy-making. They include "social partnership" (*Sozialpartnerschaft* in German/Austrian terminology, sometimes called "class struggle on the bargaining table"), "tripartism", "corporatism" or "neo-corporatism" (in the terms of Schmitter and Lehmbruch, 1979, Streeck and Schmitter, 1985, and Katzenstein, 1985). As the term "corporatism" is widely accepted (although the term is not undisputed) among political science and industrial relations scholars, as well as among labour economists, we will use it in this book. The term has its history and was at times used to describe trade associations in nineteenth-century Germany; it gained some notoriety during the dark years of fascism. However, it should be understood here merely as a definition of a governance system of a certain coherence in which the State delegates some of its authority to private interest organizations. It is not merely a loosely knit relationship between unequal partners which can be broken at any moment, but a relationship that has developed the stronger ties of a democratic governance system. As discussed in the following pages, this has resulted in delivering efficiency and equity, and backs up political stability. Corporatist governance relies on all these elements together: bipartite and tripartite concertation, tripartite policy formulation and implementation through bargaining, and even the tripartite (or bipartite) administration of institutions.

Historically, an insufficiently developed social dialogue contributed to the employment crisis in the early 1980s. At that time social dialogue experienced problems, and the approach was often more adversarial and ideologically charged. However, when it became more pragmatic and oriented towards problem solving, it contributed significantly to employment success. A new concerted effort by governments and the social partners to tackle the outstanding problems that had afflicted Europe in the 1980s and early 1990s, such as weak competitiveness and a worsening employment situation, has finally allowed some countries to emerge from the crisis.

In three of the countries under review, such a concerted effort is witnessed by the conclusion of social pacts: the first was concluded in 1982 in the Netherlands (the Wassenaar Agreement), followed by the "Declaration of Intent" in Denmark and the "Programme for National Recovery" in Ireland, both signed in 1987. The pacts expressed the desire of the partners to cooperate in order to solve the problems facing the economy through a concerted approach based on wage moderation and a boost in competitiveness, while maintaining but reforming the Welfare State. Concerted action between the social partners and the Government has been the traditional way of governance in Austria, and no new pact has been concluded. There, too, however, the system was confronted with new challenges, such as the privatization of the nationalized industries or the reform of social security.

While in other countries, such as the United Kingdom and New Zealand, the crisis ended in the dismantling of much of the existing social dialogue and its institutions, in the countries under review the song of the "sirens of deregulation" (Alan, 1997) actually had the effect of reinvigorating social dialogue. The governments in these countries usually took a leading role in bringing the partners together and in designing reform plans.

Coordination of bargaining

Conditions for conducting social dialogue are: first, strong and relatively equal partners, including trade unions and employers' organizations that are able to control their respective rank and file; and, secondly, governments as active and supporting partners. (Indeed, in the "shared public space" (Crouch, 1993) of corporatist governance, all three partners are important.) Thirdly, it is essential to have institutions in which a dialogue can take place such as the Dutch Economic and Social Council (SER) and the Labour Foundation (STAR), the Irish National Economic and Social Council (NESC) and the Central Review Committee (CRC), or the Austrian "*Paritätische Kommission*".

In order to lead to efficient macroeconomic outcomes, not only must there be partners to dialogue, but their interaction must also be coordinated. Such coordination is equally important between and within the partner organizations. For example, not only is the degree of centralization of (wage) bargaining decisive, but also the degree of coordination of bargaining. If coordination is ignored in models which try to explain the outcome of wage bargaining, highly centralized and highly decentralized bargaining seems to be efficient, while moderately decentralized systems (such as those prevailing in Denmark and the Netherlands) produce only poor outcomes (Calmfors and Driffill, 1988). If coordination is taken into consideration, however, moderately decentralized but highly coordinated bargaining also produces fair outcomes (Traxler et al., 1996).

Common elements, but national diversity

All four countries exhibit different variants of the corporatist governance model, in which the State devolves some of its prerogatives to the social partners in the "shared public space". In all four, consultation of the social partners in policy formulation and collective bargaining, as well as the administration of some labour market and social policies, is part of the overall governance system. To use the term coined by Hirschmann (1970), usually "voice" (for example, claims channelled through unions) is preferred to "exit" (refusal to compromise and acceptance of social unrest); a dialogue with the goal of reaching something like a "joint utility function" is part of the "game" of corporatist governance. However, although there are basic similarities and also a certain convergence towards a common European model, the national models of social partnership in the four countries differ (table 3.10).

The Danish model of industrial relations belongs to what is sometimes termed "Northern corporatism", which stands for highly organized and disciplined partners, intensive coordination and low level of conflict, and a facilitating (and less regulating) role of the State, which acts also as an "employer of first resort", that is to say that the right to work is implemented

Table 3.10. Models of industrial relations in Western Europe

	Northern corporatism	Central social partnership	Anglo-Saxon pluralism	Latin confrontation
Organized interests (unions and employers)	Cohesive Disciplined Comprehensive	Segmented Disciplined Partial/stable	Fragmented Volatile Variable	Rivalry Volatile Variable
Relationship	Labour-led/ balanced	Balanced/ employer-led	Alternating/ unstable	Weakness both sides/large role for the State
Wage bargaining				
– Dominant level	Sector	Sector	Company	Alternating
– Coverage	High	Medium to high	Small to moderate	Medium to high
– Depth	Significant	Moderate	Significant	Limited
– Style	Integrative	Integrative	Adversarial	Contestational
– Pattern	Stable	Stable	Unstable	Unstable
Coordination	Considerable	Considerable	Absent	Variable
Conflict	Medium to low Highly organized	Low Highly organized	Medium to high Dispersed	High Spasmodic
Role of the State	Facilitating	Facilitating and regulating	Abstaining	Intervening
	Collective labour rights	Individual and collective labour rights	Voluntarism	Individual and collective labour rights
Welfare State	Comprehensive Right to work	Fragmented Right to income	Residual –	Rudimentary Right to work and welfare proclaimed
	State is employer of first resort	State is compensator of first resort	State is enforcer of work in market-place	–
Countries	Sweden Finland **Denmark** Norway	**Austria** Germany Switzerland Belgium **Netherlands**	United Kingdom **Ireland**	France Italy Spain Portugal Greece

Source: Visser (forthcoming).

through a high share of public sector jobs and active labour market policy. Austria and the Netherlands stand for the "Central European Social Partnership", sometimes also termed the "Rhineland model" (Albert, 1993), with similar characteristics, but with a more regulating role played by the State. Government institutes a "right to income", while the "employer of first resort" principle changes into a principle of a "compensator of first resort", focusing more on organizing income replacement than providing jobs. Finally, Ireland belongs traditionally to the Anglo-Saxon pluralist

Table 3.11. Working days lost through industrial action per 1,000 employed, selected EU countries and United States, 1980–96 (annual averages)

Country	1980–89		1990–96	
	Days	Rank	Days	Rank
Austria	2	20	5	21
Denmark	178	12	43	16
Ireland	380	7	132	9
Netherlands	15	18	29	19
Germany[1]	28	17	17	20
France	119	15	87	12
United Kingdom	332	9	37	18
United States	123	14	44	15

Notes: The above is a selection from a table in which countries are ranked from 1 (Italy being the most strike-prone country) to 23 (Switzerland being the country with the lowest strike rate). [1] Until 1993 only West Germany.

Source: iw-trends 1/98.

model, with fragmented interests, no or very low coordination and accordingly a comparatively high rate of labour conflicts.

Recent strike figures show that while conflicts have decreased in all countries, the above patterns seem at least partially to prevail among the four countries compared, with Ireland still having the highest strike activity measured by lost working days for 1,000 employed (table 3.11).

Rankings of corporatism, which usually stress factors such as centralization of bargaining, union density, interaction with government, bargaining coverage, and so on, normally show Austria as the most corporatist country of Europe. Denmark is generally considered to be more corporatist than the Netherlands, or equally so, while Ireland is usually found at the bottom of the European scale as one of the least corporatist countries.

Limitation of typologies

While such typologies as outlined above are useful to grasp the complex realities of industrial relations and some of their outcomes, they have at least two shortcomings. First, all attempts to categorize country models in "ideal types" are inadequate in capturing the complexity of the issues involved. Secondly, it is difficult to separate structure from recent trends. Structures resulting from past developments are clearly affected by recent changes; a judgement based on the latter leads to different results than one based on the former. For analytical purposes, the typology can still serve as a frame of reference, but never as a concise picture of reality. For example, although it is true that conflicts (measured by lost working days) tend to be still higher in Ireland than in the three other countries, the reality of industrial relations, the Welfare State and labour market policy there has indeed dramatically changed. The social pacts (which started in 1987, and continue today) are a good illustration of this new reality, as they have required, for example, a higher degree of coordination than in the past and a changed role of the government as a facilitator of collective bargaining. This can be interpreted as a convergence towards the Nordic and central social partnership model, which is not least to be seen as a consequence of Ireland joining the EU. This has reduced the importance of the traditional Anglo-Saxon tradition of voluntarism, company bargaining, demarcation and conflicts.

The four countries also represent divergent trends in union density (share of union members among the workforce), employer "density" (share of workers whose firms belong to employers' organizations) and collective bargaining coverage rates (share of workers covered by collective agreements). In the wake of the dramatic sectoral shifts in employment from the highly unionized manufacturing sector to the less unionized service sector, and the deregulation policies of the 1990s, unions have in general lost members (ILO, 1997). Denmark seems to have escaped the trend, probably because unions run the unemployment funds, which gives an additional incentive for workers to join. While union membership was declining in the Netherlands during the 1980s, membership has been growing again lately.

The extent of union and employer density and the coverage by collective bargaining contracts for European countries in the mid-1990s are shown in table 3.12.

In Denmark, high union density rates go together with low to medium employer density and a medium to low level of bargaining coverage. With markedly lower union density, but the same employer density as Denmark, Ireland has approximately the same coverage rate. Austria has relatively high and the Netherlands has low union density rates, and the employer density rate is about the same, but both have high coverage rates. High coverage rates might be a consequence of legal mechanisms to extend collective bargaining agreements, as both Austrian and Dutch labour legislation provide for such possibilities.

Between decentralization and Europeanization

All "models" of social dialogue and industrial relations have been subject to change in recent years. One important factor is the trend towards "organized decentralization" (Visser, forthcoming), that is to say, the displacement of bargaining from central to intermediate (branch, company) levels, while usually retaining macroeconomic coordination. Countries are differently positioned in this regard: for example, in Austria decentralized bargaining has been more cautiously implemented than in Denmark or in the Netherlands.

Table 3.12. Coverage of trade unions, employers' organizations and collective agreements, Western European countries

Country	% workers belonging to trade unions	% workers in firms belonging to the main employers' organizations	% workers covered by collective agreements	Extension of agreements through public law	National minimum wage
Sweden	77	60	72	Absent	Agreement
Finland	65	58	67	Limited	Agreement
Denmark	**68**	**48**	**52**	**Absent**	**Agreement**
Norway	45	54	62	Negligible	Agreement
Belgium	40	80	82	Significant	Statutory (69%)
Austria	**37**	**96**	**97**	**Significant**	**Agreement**
Germany	25	76	80	Limited	Agreement
Switzerland	18	37	50	Limited	Agreement
Netherlands	**19**	**80**	**79**	**Limited**	**Statutory (60%)**
Ireland	**37**	**44**	**n.a.**	**Negligible**	**(Industry councils)**
Great Britain	21	57	40	Absent	No
Italy	32	40	n.a.	Absent	Agreement
France	<7	71	75	Significant	Statutory (73%)
Spain	<15	70	67	Limited	Statutory (40%)
Portugal	<20	n.a.	n.a.	Limited	Statutory (70%)
Greece	<15	n.a.	n.a.	Significant	Statutory (57%)
Average	36	62	69		

Source: Visser (forthcoming).

Another change is the addition of new bargaining issues, such as training, work organization, leave schemes, social security reforms (e.g. pensions and early retirement), working time and employment issues (employment maintenance), which has led to an extended bargaining agenda.

National industrial relations patterns are subject not only to national, but increasingly also to European developments. European directives such as the Working-Time Directive, the Posted Workers Directive or the Directive regulating European Works Councils are one factor, and the European Employment Strategy is another. While the directives usually do not have a strong impact on countries with "fully fledged" corporatism, as there such issues have already been regulated, the impact on a country such as Ireland is more important. For example, when bargaining at company level, corporatist governance features such as works councils are an asset. Particularly in this regard, Irish institutions are weakly developed, as social dialogue is usually conducted at central level. The European Works Councils Directive or any future directive that establishes information, consultation or even co-determination rights at the company level through a European company statute could be a driving force for the installation of such structures.

Moreover, European efforts to adapt and promote social dialogue at community level should be mentioned as a driving force of the dialogue (European Commission, 1998a).

The European Employment Strategy, to whose elaboration national social partners have been contributing, has some impact, at least on the outcomes of national bargaining and on social partner institutions such as employment services. In particular, the drafting of "national action plans" for employment policies gives the social partners new insights and rights to intervene in national employment and labour market policies. In the wake of the Strategy, "the right to income" could in future be increasingly replaced by "a right to work" or at least "a right to activation" in all four countries (European Commission, 1998f).

The contribution of social dialogue to employment success

The crucial question for this study is whether and how social dialogue and national systems of industrial relations have contributed to relative employment success. This contribution can be summarized by three main factors: moderate wage increases, a low incidence of industrial conflict and support for sometimes unpopular reforms.

Wage moderation

Wage moderation was the core target of the social pacts in Denmark, Ireland and the Netherlands, and is a long-standing feature of the Austrian system. In the absence of understanding between the social partners, a wage/price inflation spiral afflicted many European countries in the late 1970s and 1980s. Wage and price inflation has, however, come down to low levels in the 1990s, a remarkable outcome due not least to policies of wage moderation hammered out as part of social dialogue (see figures 3.1 and 3.2). Declining inflation was not exclusive to countries with social dialogue, but occurred in most OECD and EU countries. At declining rates of inflation, due among other factors to a tight monetary policy (but also trade liberalization and productivity advances), a moderate wage policy is more easily maintained. In fact, a virtuous circle of wage restraint, low inflation and declines in unit labour costs has fuelled the economies of all four countries.

Real wage growth was also moderate, but usually not negative, at least after 1985/86. It was more moderate in the Netherlands and Denmark than in Austria or Ireland (see figure 3.3).

In addition, wage differentials seem not to have dramatically increased, although countries differ in that regard, and controversy persists as poor data on the subject leave room for divergent interpretations. Income inequality measured as the distribution of GDP per head show that income is much more evenly distributed in Austria and Denmark than in the Netherlands

Figure 3.1.   Consumer prices, annual rates of change, 1980–98 (percentages)

Percentages

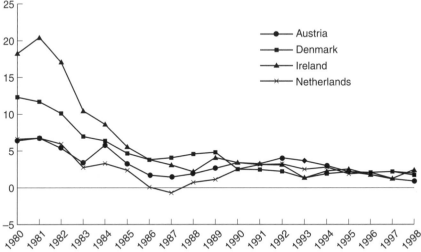

Source: OECD: *Economic Outlook*, Dec.1998.

Figure 3.2.   Compensation per employee, annual rates of change, 1980–98 (percentages)

Percentages

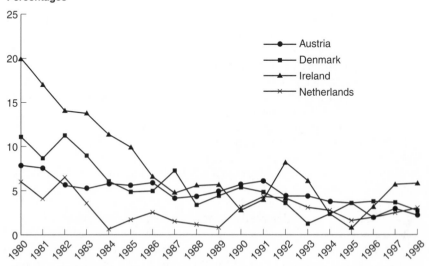

Source: OECD: *Economic Outlook*, Dec. 1998.

Figure 3.3. Real compensation per employee, 1980–98 (1980 = 100)

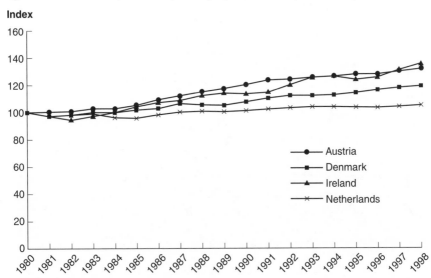

Source: OECD: *Economic Outlook*, Dec.1998.

and Ireland (see Annex I). However, Pichelmann , with Hofer (1999), note that Austria has traditionally high wage differentials between and within sectors, which have not declined. Hartog (1999) shows for the Netherlands that there is more wage inequality today than in the 1980s, and O'Connell (1999) notes that while substantial improvements in the material living standards of workers have been achieved in Ireland, this has coincided with an increase in inequality. On the contrary, Danish unions have engaged in a "solidaristic" wage policy along Swedish lines which has resulted in low wage dispersion, a trend that has been maintained.

It is difficult to reach clear conclusions on wage inequality, but it seems that recent job growth has actually led to greater inequality, at least in the countries with the largest job increases. There are various reasons for this, such as the lowering of the minimum wage in the Netherlands, the growing incidence of low-paid jobs in Ireland, and more general change in employment systems towards greater heterogeneity. It seems that while European wage trends have not created as much inequality in the distribution of income as the decentralized system of the United States (see figure 3.4 and Annex I for some comparative measures), recently in some countries (e.g. Ireland, and to a more limited extent also the Netherlands) rising inequality has accompanied job growth. A marked difference from the United States is that apparently no longer-term real wage decreases were accepted under European wage policy, although real wages did not show a positive trend in every year after 1985

61

Figure 3.4. Trends in real earnings dispersion, D9/D1,[1] both sexes: Comparison
with the United States, 1980–94

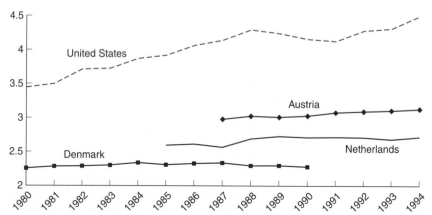

Note: [1]Ninth over first decile in real earnings distribution.
Source: OECD: *Economic Outlook*, Dec. 1997.

(see figure 3.2). A tentative conclusion is that a somewhat better balance
between efficiency and equity concerns seems to be one outcome of wage
policy under corporatist governance.

In conclusion, while other countries without corporatist governance also
experienced low inflation and low wage growth, this usually went together
with real wage declines (at least for large parts of the employed), and led to
faster-growing wage disparity than in countries with corporatist governance.
It should be also noted that wage moderation generally went hand in hand
with tax cuts, and in some countries also with working-time reductions.
Such "package deals" consisting of moderate wages and tax cuts had the
beneficial effect of maintaining disposable income despite lower gross wages,
and thus supported domestic demand.

Reforms in social security and the labour market

The new macroeconomic responsibility of the social partners resulting from
the social pacts has also led to low levels of industrial conflict (see table 3.4).
This is all the more remarkable as they were engaged in unpopular reforms
of the social security system. During the discussions on reform, the unions,
in particular, had to slaughter some sacred cows, and industrial conflict
could easily have arisen from low wage agreements and welfare reforms.
Tight public budgets, authorized not least by the requirement to meet the
Maastricht convergence criteria, have required such reforms. But these
reforms also entail a new distribution of responsibility between the State,
employers and workers.

The privatization of the nationalized sector in Austria during the 1980s, as well as the recent reform of social security, including old-age pensions, within the framework of the austerity package, can be cited as examples. Both reforms were difficult to swallow for the unions: the state-owned industrial sector (mainly steel and chemicals), a union stronghold, had run into structural problems. Its successful restructuring showed that within the social partnership trade unions could also deal with problems affecting their members. Unions bargained for accompanying measures such as early retirement and the *Stahlstiftungen*, a new employment policy instrument for training and placement of redundant workers. The recent conclusion of the austerity package, a bundle of budget consolidation measures, is another proof that social partnership is able to deal with difficult issues.

In the Netherlands, too, the social partners have repeatedly shown that they are not just administrators of acquired rights, but an active part of a reform process which sometimes cuts deeply into vested interests. Again, the Government has been very active in convincing unions and employers to begin bargaining and to accept reforms. The reform of the sickness benefit system is one illustration of this: in two steps, sickness benefit administration has been made the responsibility of employers. First, employers were made responsible for the payment of the first six weeks of their employees' sickness, and then this compensation was extended to cover the first year of sickness. Employers' contributions to health insurance were accordingly cut. This reform shows how the Dutch Government implements reforms in which the social partners have a say: while the benefit level is regulated by law, the implementation of policies is mandated to the social partners or at least to one of them. The idea is that such a system will lead the partners to assume more responsibilities (and costs if the system is disproportionally used) and will ultimately result in a more cost-effective system in which prevention of (health) risks plays a large role. Similar regulations, introducing a sort of "experience rating" (those using the system more often have to pay higher contributions), will apply to the invalidity system. It remains to be seen if such changes will lead to the expected results. There seem to be some drawbacks as well: as far as health insurance is concerned, employers have resorted to health checks on hiring, which has led to government intervention to forbid such checks. Also, company doctors seem to be under more pressure to disclose information on the health situation of employees, and the prevention packages offered to employers by private insurance companies seem not to have been taken up on a large scale (EIRO news).

In Denmark, several labour market policy reforms have been enacted with the help of the social partners: initially, unemployment benefit duration was cut from seven to five years, providing for an "activation period" after the first two years (six months for unqualified youth); a further reform foresees a maximum duration of four years, with an advanced activation period. Under the reform adopted by Parliament, a job or active measure has to be accepted after one year (three months for youth), which means that Denmark has implemented some targets of the European Employment Strategy. The second "pillar" of the retirement system – a contribution-based system – to supplement the tax-financed basic pension, has been extended and plays a role in wage bargaining (trade-offs between pension contributions and wage increases in some sectors), as does the question of early retirement.

In Ireland, alongside the various social pacts, joint committees on a series of reform areas were set up, and have led to social partner involvement in issues such as social security and labour market reforms, as well as equality of opportunity policies.

Another important point on the agenda of the social partners has been working time. In all four countries, in particular Austria, Denmark and the Netherlands, substantial reductions in contractual hours have taken place, while labour laws usually provided for more flexibility of working time. Although individual working time was reduced, equipment running time and shop opening hours were extended through flexible working time and work organization patterns. However, countries still differ in the broad picture of their working-time distribution (see Bosch, forthcoming), as well as in the ways in which they have arrived at low effective working time. In the Netherlands this was achieved mainly through an extension of part-time work. In Denmark effective hours have been reduced also through leave schemes, while in Austria this occurred mainly through a reduction in regular weekly working hours. The employment effects of working-time reductions are the subject of controversy, but Bosch (op. cit.) shows that they have generally been positive. However, part of the effect was compensated for by an increase in productivity.

Some problems with corporatist governance

The examples cited show that the social partners have been active in the reforms of the different policy fields and have taken on new responsibilities which sometimes entail substantial changes for their constituents, against a background of a low level of open conflict. However, the changes were not implemented without conflicts and hard, at times controversial, bargaining. In Austria many complaints have been expressed about cumbersome discussions between the social partners, and reforms have been criticized for being too hesitant. Overt conflicts might yet accompany reforms: for example, the influential unskilled workers' union SID has not accepted the latest step of the Danish labour market reform (a cut in the duration of the unemployment benefit period to four years and "activation" after one year) (EIRO news).

In general, corporatist governance procedures can be lengthy and controversial, and many compromises have to be found. Governments have taken a leading role in reforms and negotiations, sometimes with the threat of unilateral legislation if agreement is not reached. The social partners have also been accused of sometimes following self-interested policies which are not always of public benefit. Such accusations have been heard especially in relation to early labour market exit measures. For example, in the Netherlands, but also in Austria, the use of invalidity pensions for exits on labour market grounds, encouraged by the social partners, has been criticized. Again in the Netherlands, the administration of the public employment service by the partners has been criticized by an evaluation report (Dercksen and de Koning, 1996).

In Denmark the last pay bargaining round was ended by government intervention, because of the refusal by the union rank and file of the compromise agreed between the social partners at national level. The latter conflict shows at least two things of general importance. First, the social partners have to establish close contacts with their rank and file in order to ensure that the bargaining outcomes are honoured. Secondly, during the bargaining round it was revealed that there was a lack of discussion between the two partners between bargaining rounds, and that their positions had been far apart. Moreover, no central social dialogue has been conducted, owing to the lack of bipartite consultation committees at that level. In the meantime such a committee has been created (EIRO news). In this regard, the existing institutions for social dialogue in other countries have been shown to be of major importance for corporatist governance.

Conclusion

Corporatist governance, the system which has been established in three of the four countries (the fourth, Ireland, being on its way towards such a system), implies a joint venture in economic and, in particular, labour and social affairs between the social partners and the government. While the government is democratically authorized to run all affairs in a country in the public interest, employers' and workers' organizations are authorized by their constituents to represent their specific interests. It is only through repeated rounds of social dialogue that the public interest and the interest of the social partners can be made compatible. Conditions for the dialogue are equal partners and a will to compromise in order to reach outcomes which are acceptable to all. Because bargaining rounds are repeated, unequal outcomes in one round can (and will) be corrected in following rounds. Therefore, the "shadow of the future" (Axelrod, 1984) usually leads the social partners to acceptable outcomes. Of course, regulations such as an obligatory or voluntary "peace obligation" during the validity of collective agreements bar partners from too frequent renegotiations of terms.

However, different forms of social dialogue exist: the dialogue concerning the "state of the world" (Visser, forthcoming) between the main organizations and the State sets the framework for dialogue on other levels, declares the intentions and capabilities of each partner and promotes trust in mutual commitments. This level of social concertation was decisive for the change in the economic and social climate which finally led to today's outcomes. How-ever, the dialogue needs to have other levels as well, from central negotiations to company bargaining, and especially at more concrete implementation levels. As with all truly democratic processes, the social dialogue might some-times appear to be cumbersome, difficult and lengthy. However, the chance that its results will be accepted and defended by a majority is also much greater than in any other form of governance.

Acceptable achievements for all, or excellence for a few?

Social dialogue is also vulnerable, however: it does not aim at the most efficient outcome for a minority, but at an outcome acceptable to a majority. That is, social dialogue tends to settle on a medium level of results for all, and not the maximum outcome for a few. This is why it can always be attacked in the name of other ways of governance that are supposed to be more efficient.

The most prominent alternative to corporatist government is seen today in market forces. The unbridled interplay of market forces is regarded as a more efficient allocation instrument than the visible hand of corporatist governance. However, as can be seen from comparative rankings in efficiency and equity (see Annex I), it might well be that the market is a better instrument to achieve good results for a few, but it is certain that there is no better instrument for achieving acceptable results for as many as possible than a developed form of corporatist governance. While this form of governance cannot totally avoid rising inequalities, these do remain more limited, and it seems that generally corporatism has prevented real wage declines. Such real wage declines and strong income inequalities have accompanied most market-led approaches, despite their sometimes superior employment performance.

In general, employment performance – as measured by employment growth, and employment and unemployment rates – is the "Achilles heel" of Europe. If its employment problem could be solved, Europe would outper-form all other existing economic systems if efficiency *and* equity considerations were taken into account. This said, some of the smaller countries of Europe are on their way to full employment and are already among the highest-ranking countries in terms of efficiency, equity and labour market performance. This does not mean that all problems have been solved: inequalities seem to have risen as well, and these need to be addressed, while exclusion and even poverty for a minority are problems which still await policy solutions.

Besides being superior in income distribution (and by the way, superior also in productivity growth, and at least equal and sometimes even superior in terms of wealth creation, not to speak of leisure time – see Annex I), corporatist governance (based on a market economy) is also more stable than market governance. While the countries which have opted for a relatively free market approach tend to be more dynamic in creating jobs, they tend also to be more dynamic in destroying them. Even if on balance they create more jobs, there is a much greater individual probability of job loss, leading to a strong feeling of job and income insecurity.

In contrast, corporatist governance systems tend to smooth the cyclical swings of economic and even political developments. In an economic crisis, transfer benefits are made available and institutions are used to stabilize employment. In political terms, corporatist interest organizations are an element of stability, as they survive transient governments and prevent radical political change. In addition, corporatist governance, which implies that many problems are solved and many policy areas administered by the social partners themselves, can also lead to "leaner" governments. In a recent conference on social dialogue, the social partnership system was described as an element of "comfort" for governments, as they are freed of responsibility for many regulatory actions.

It is true that there can be a feeling of "fatigue" about institutions which have been in existence for many years and are apparently unchangeable. This seems to be the case in Austria, where social partnership has been in place for 50 years. However, tremendous changes have been made with the help of this "rigid" system of governance. This feeling does not yet exist in the countries which have undergone a major crisis and which have succeeded in ending it through a renewed social pact, because the benefits of corporatist governance are more visible when a troublesome past is not too remote.

LABOUR MARKET POLICIES

In order to influence unemployment and employment more directly, the governments and social partners of all four countries have made use of labour market policy. Indeed, passive and active labour market policies are among the few instruments in the tool kits of policy-makers which enable a direct impact to be made on the labour market, as they allow for job search and job matches, supply enhancement and reduction, and the creation of additional jobs, while generally providing replacement income. In passive labour market policies the claimants are in general required not to be involved in any activity, neither employed nor involved in an active measure – but available and actively searching for work – whereas active policies always require those receiving benefits to participate in either work or training activities.[1] While "passive" income replacement programmes include unemployment insurance benefits and all other benefits such as early retirement benefits paid on the condition of not being active, active policies comprise a wide range of measures acting both on the supply and the demand side of the labour market.

Passive labour market policies

In this study we address some issues of general interest such as the "generosity" of the unemployment benefit system and its trade-off with employment protection, flexibility aspects of income-replacement schemes, and the question of early retirement and its contribution to relative employment success. Moreover, some issues linked to active labour market policies and "activation" policies, as well as aspects of public employment service reforms, are also discussed.

In the 1970s, unemployment was still considered to be caused by temporary mismatches in the labour market and temporary periods of insufficient demand. Thus the basic function of unemployment benefit systems was temporary income provision to allow job search or to weather cyclical troughs. This has changed since the 1980s: unemployment benefit systems have had to face increased structural change as a consequence of shifts in the sectoral distribution of employment, technological and organizational change, and globalization, which together have led to continuous downsizing in traditional parts of the economy and rising employment in new sectors. This results in prolonged periods of insufficient labour demand and mismatches of supply and demand, that is, structural demand deficiencies. Supply-side restrictions, such as inappropriate or outdated skills and disincentives for labour mobility, also play a role. In economic theory, however, structural features were no longer considered relevant to labour demand, but almost exclusively to labour supply. For example, concerning unemployment benefit systems, the "generosity" of income replacement and duration of benefit payments came to be seen not as protecting workers against prolonged periods of income losses, but as a major cause of unemployment, particularly long-term unemployment.

A good description of some of the evidence on the effects of the benefit system on unemployment is given by Graafland (1996). The conclusion here is that it does have an effect on the persistence of unemployment, and that duration of benefits, rather than benefit levels, account for most of this effect. Such results seem plausible and draw attention to a simple fact: if it is legally possible to draw benefits for a long period, this should result in a longer (registered) duration of unemployment, as long as the cause of unemployment (e.g. insufficient offers of acceptable jobs) persists. Clearly, in unemployment systems, which offer benefits only for a short period (e.g. six months), registered long-duration unemployment can by definition not occur.[2] It is hard to prove this with the available information on replacement rates and unemployment duration in the four countries, however. In all four of them it is possible to draw benefits for a long period, at least as far as unemployment assistance is concerned. One cannot deny that there is an (usually) unknown percentage of misuse in the system and that generous systems alleviate the pressures to immediately accept work of any kind. In fact, such systems were also established to allow better job matching, which is always more difficult in periods of high unemployment. The litmus test for assumptions that the "generosity" of the unemployment insurance system is a more than marginal cause of long-duration unemployment is a

Table 3.13. Unemployment benefit replacement rates, 1994, and duration of benefits, 1997 (percentages)

Replacement rate		Duration
		Austria
1.	57/69	Depending on insured employment and age: 20 weeks to 52 weeks
2.	–/78	Assistance: unlimited subject to means test
3.	58/74	
4.	–/100	
		Denmark
1.	69/73	5 years (activation measures after 2 years)
2.	–/83	From Jan. 1999: 4 years (activation measures after 1 year)
3.	92/93	
4.	–/95	
		Ireland
1.	49/64	390 days
2.	–/64	Assistance: unlimited subject to means test
3.	67/70	
4.	–/70	
		Netherlands
1.	77/77	General benefits: 6 months
2.	–/80	Extended: depending on age and duration of insured employment
3.	79/78	From 9 months to 5 years
4	–/95	Follow-up benefits: 2 years

Notes: Net replacement rates for single-earner households, 1994: 1. Couple, no children/2 children, 1 month of unemployment, as a percentage of average production worker income. 2. Couple, no children/2 children, 60 months of unemployment, average production worker income. 3. Couple, no children/2 children, but at two-thirds of average production worker income and including social assistance. 4. Couple, no children/2 children, but two-thirds of average production worker income, and including social assistance.

Source: OECD.

sustained recovery on the job market without a similar improvement in, for example, the Beveridge (or unemployment vacancy) curve.

Based on the evidence from the four countries (table 3.13), the assumed generosity of the benefit system does not easily provide empirical evidence for more than a marginal impact on unemployment in the longer term: if we take the cases of Austria and Ireland, we see that the Austrian system is more generous for most categories than the Irish, while (subject to means testing) benefits can be drawn indefinitely in both systems. Despite this, Ireland has much higher long-term unemployment rates. If we compare the Netherlands and Denmark, with the same replacement rates for those with long periods of unemployment, we have also a starkly contrasting picture: Denmark has low long-term unemployment rates, but the Netherlands still faces high rates.

We could extend this argument to different regions in one country: here at least we can assume that national replacement and duration rates do not vary by region and can therefore not be held responsible for any differences in long-term unemployment rates. However, these rates differ also by regions, suggesting that other explanations, such as the extent of structural change, are important. An additional point is that women are usually less covered by benefits than men (e.g. because of more difficult access to benefits because of more heterogeneous career paths) and only in Denmark do women reach a high coverage share (Rubery, forthcoming).

Nevertheless, many smaller (administrative) reforms have been undertaken in unemployment protection systems in almost all the countries under review, some of which have also produced the intended effect. One or more of the following changes have been enacted: either the duration of benefits and/or the level of wage replacement rates were cut and/or eligibility was restricted. In addition, all countries resorted to a much stricter enforcement of job search and suitable work provisions. That is to say, in different ways in different countries, access to and duration of benefits have been restricted and sanctions tightened. Some of these restrictions had an impact on the decline in unemployment, which is, however, difficult to measure. In Denmark, for example, restriction on the access of poorly educated youth to benefits by linking benefit payments to an obligatory participation in education had a tangible effect on youth unemployment. However, this is much more a policy of activation (as it compensates restrictions on the passive side with offers on the active side), and in the light of the above it seems that in general policies of activation are more promising than administrative changes alone.

Flexibility and security in unemployment benefit systems

One explanation for differences in the dimension of long-term unemployment beyond the traditional generosity/duration argument could be the high turnover of the unemployed in both Austria and Denmark, both countries with low rates and shares of long-term unemployment. In Austria, for example, around 700,000 persons register for unemployment each year, but the stock remains around the 200,000 level. Annual stocks and flows into unemployment stand in a relation of about 1:3.5 in Austria and 1:2 in Denmark, but were (at least in 1994) almost equal (registered unemployment) in the Netherlands (no data for Ireland) (OECD data, 1996). This might change over time, but high shares of long-term unemployment and a concentration of the unemployed in the longer-duration brackets (see table 3.14) suggest a much lower mobility of the unemployed in the Netherlands, and also in Ireland.

To some extent this is explained by high seasonal unemployment in Austria and by the fact that Denmark traditionally runs a sort of lay-off system, combining low employment protection with high social protection. In Austria such lay-off behaviour, with frequent recalls, also seems to spread beyond the seasonal sectors. It is estimated that around 30 per cent of the unemployed have a commitment to take up a job with the same employer after their

Table 3.14. Duration of unemployment, 1992 and 1996 (percentages)

Duration of employment	Austria		Denmark		Ireland		Netherlands		EU 15	
	1992	1996	1992	1996	1992	1996	1992	1996	1992	1996
Less than 6 months	n.a.	57.5	50.1	55.6	22.6	24.3	23.1	18.6	n.a.	33.2
Men	n.a.	61.8	51.2	55.8	20.1	20.8	25.2	18.8	n.a.	35.3
Women	n.a.	51.9	49.0	55.4	27.2	29.9	21.6	18.5	n.a.	31.0
Of which less than 3 months	n.a.	29.2	31.7	37.2	11.1	14.3	11.0	9.4	n.a.	n.a.
Men	n.a.	30.9	31.8	36.0	9.5	10.5	14.7	8.9	n.a.	n.a.
Women	n.a.	28.6	31.7	39.8	14.0	15.4	10.5	9.9	n.a.	n.a.
6 to 11 months	n.a.	16.8	22.9	17.9	18.5	16.2	32.9	32.4	n.a.	18.6
Men	n.a.	15.0	23.4	16.1	16.8	14.6	27.8	27.7	n.a.	18.4
Women	n.a.	19.3	22.5	19.3	21.5	18.9	36.8	36.6	n.a.	18.8
12 months and more	n.a.	25.6	27.0	26.5	58.9	59.5	44.0	49.0	n.a.	48.2
Men	n.a.	23.2	25.3	28.1	63.1	64.6	47.0	53.5	n.a.	46.3
Women	n.a.	28.8	28.5	25.3	51.3	51.2	41.6	45.0	n.a.	50.2
24 months and more	n.a.	13.4	8.8	11.6	39.2	41.1	27.7	33.7	n.a.	30.0
Men	n.a.	13.1	6.9	12.3	44.9	47.4	31.7	37.9	n.a.	28.7
Women	n.a.	13.7	10.6	11.0	29.0	31.0	24.6	29.9	n.a.	31.5

n.a. = not available.
Source: ILO CEPR data bank based on Eurostat (LTS) data.

unemployment spell (Frühstück et al., 1998). In lay-off systems (and unemployment systems with a large seasonal component) there is a sort of implicit contract between employers, their workers and unemployment compensation institutions, which allows companies to shift their labour costs in quiet seasons or in temporary declines of demand to unemployment compensation systems. Those laid off are rehired once demand picks up again or the active season begins.

Such a mutual use of the unemployment benefit system supports labour market flexibility while ensuring a security network for the workers, albeit at a certain cost to unemployment protection systems. It might also allow firms to keep an experienced workforce and might thus be productivity enhancing. This depends not least on how recurrent unemployment is. In Austria, for example, individuals experienced on average 1.3 spells of unemployment per annum, indicating some recurrence linked to this particular system. However, other job openings also seem to be available in these systems, as not all of those laid off return to the same employer who has laid them off. In Denmark, labour market policy has contributed to short-duration unemployment.

The flexible use of the unemployment insurance system seems to have positive effects on the employment rate as well: both Denmark and Austria have higher employment-to-population ratios than the two other countries and a larger share of the unemployed had held a job before becoming unemployed.[3]

Lay-off procedures involving a "joint venture" of all partners concerned could therefore also be one of the explanations for relatively good labour market performance, that is, a high labour turnover, combined with high participation rates and low long-duration unemployment. In Austria, for example, the high turnover in the unemployment system is mirrored by high employment turnover with around 1 million entries and 1 million exits each year for a labour force of 3.8 million.

More traditional use of the unemployment compensation system prevails in Ireland and the Netherlands. In such systems the seasonal and temporary lay-off component is smaller, with more long-term unemployment. Such systems go together with lower employment rates and higher entry unemployment (e.g. for the young), and less employment turnover.

However, while the social partners might find a lay-off system satisfactory (especially in small firms), there are also critics of the system who point to the costs for others. Concentrated use of unemployment funds by certain sectors, such as agriculture, construction, or hotels and catering, leads to cross-subsidization, especially in contribution-financed unemployment insurance systems. Seasonal unemployment is made more viable, and the OECD (1998a) has pointed out that high seasonal unemployment is indeed a problem in Austria.

Cross-subsidization could be addressed by introducing experience rating which, however, would have a bearing on labour costs that could negatively affect hiring decisions, especially in low-wage sectors. Also as a tentative measure, useful employment alternatives might be developed in "dead" seasons. Working-time flexibility can also be an alternative: in Austria, the social partners have, for example, recently agreed on the introduction of a working-time pattern which has the effect of prolonging the season in the construction industry by an annualization of working time (compensation of overtime in leisure rather than in money, and an obligation to take a part of holidays during the dead season). However, while these changes might prevent the development of extreme forms of distorted use of the unemployment insurance system, the core of the system should be maintained as it provides firms with flexibility and workers with flexibility and security.

These considerations point to the fact that "passive labour market policy" is indeed conceived not only to provide income protection to workers, but also to allow flexibility, especially for small companies. Any substantial changes in the system, such as tightening access, restricting "generosity" (reducing replacement rates, introducing waiting periods, etc.), might therefore have drawbacks for labour market flexibility. For example, a recent Danish report indicates that a lowering in overall generosity (replacement rates) could lead to claims for more dismissal protection. This leads to the question whether there is a basic trade-off between dismissal protection at the firm level and social protection at the macro level, and how changes in one system might affect the other. The evidence of such a trade-off is clearly outlined in a recent

Figure 3.5. Trade-off between employment security and unemployment benefits

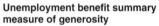

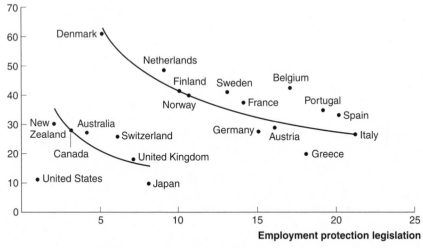

Notes: Generosity indexes and employment protection legislation scores are based on OECD data: low values indicate low "generosity" (replacement rates, duration, etc.) or low levels of employment protection (notice, severance pay, etc.). Data refer to 1985–93 for employment protection and averages for the 1990s for employment generosity. For details see also Cazes et al. (1999).

Source: Buti et al. (1998).

paper by the "forward studies unit" of the European Commission (Buti et al., 1998), which shows that there is evidence of weaker social protection going together with tighter dismissal protection, at least in European countries. These authors assume different "indifference curves" for Anglo-Saxon countries (which have generally lower generosity and lower employment protection) than for continental European countries, with higher values for both.

Such a trade-off is important for policy, as it implies a need for complex policy-making which considers both sides of the trade-off. However, more evidence is needed: figure 3.5 shows that, apart from Denmark, there seems to be not much evidence of such a trade-off. Data indicate that there is no clear-cut relationship or even a slight positive association. This would suggest that stricter employment protection is associated with stricter unemployment protection. One also has to disentangle the purely legal dimension from the de facto side. For example, despite Austria's tighter dismissal protection and lower generosity of benefits, the actual trade-off between employment protection at firm level and social protection at macro level seems to work equally well, as in Denmark. On this point, and for a critical discussion of employment protection indicators, see Cazes et al. (1999).

Exit measures for the older workforce: Early retirement and invalidity pensions

Another strand of passive policies has been heavily used to reduce supply pressure on the labour markets of all the countries under review, and has therefore contributed to keeping unemployment below the level it would have reached in the absence of such policies. Early retirement schemes and to a certain extent also invalidity pensions, when granted on labour market grounds, have been important tools to allow the exit of older workers, even in the face of particularly severe dismissal protection for older workers and/ or the special social responsibility firms have towards their long-term staff. Here we see a trade-off between dismissal protection and social protection of a different kind: the better the protection against dismissal, the more exit measures exist to allow firms to adjust their employment levels to the needs of structural change.

Early retirement has played a large role in reducing labour supply in all four countries. Invalidity pensions have also been used increasingly for labour market reasons. Both have contributed especially to the decline in employment rates of older men and have lowered the average effective pension age (see tables 3.15 and 3.16).

While early retirement has been an important tool to alleviate supply pressures on the labour market, it has also been increasingly criticized as a very costly alternative. The combined effects of workforce ageing, increased life expectancy and the trend towards ever earlier withdrawal from the labour market have required changes in early exit schemes. Pressures on public budgets have also made it necessary to restrict access to this kind of "easy exit" option, which has usually won the approval of the social partners, as well as workers and employers at the workplace level. Several changes have been introduced in the countries under review.

Austria has restricted access to early retirement by abolishing the *Sonderunterstützung*, a combination of early retirement and unemployment benefits,

Table 3.15. Employment rates for the 55–64 age group, 1985 and 1997

Country	Total		Male		Female	
	1985	1997	1985	1997	1985	1997
Austria	28.6	29.3	47.7	42.4	14.1	17.4
Denmark	51.2	52.2	63.4	62.2	40.7	42.0
Ireland	41.1	40.2	65.9	59.0	17.3	21.3
Netherlands	28.5	30.7	45.7	42.6	13.2	19.0
EU	38.0	35.9	54.3	46.6	23.6	25.9

Source: European Commission: *Employment Rates Report*, 1998.

Table 3.16. Statutory recent and effective retirement age

Country	Statutory recent		Effective			
			1970		1990	
	Male	Female	Male	Female	Male	Female
Austria	65	60[1]	62.2	60.0	58.5	56.4
Denmark	67	67	66.8	61.5	62.9	59.5
Ireland[2]	65/66	65/66	69.5	72.6	63.7	61.2
Netherlands	65	65	64.0	62.1	59.0	55.7

Notes: [1]After 2024 gradual increase to 65. [2]Age 65 for retirement pension, 66 for old-age pension.
Sources: MISSOC (1998); Latulippe (1996).

in 1996 and is further reducing the attractiveness of all early retirement possibilities (e.g. by cutting reference wages) with the aim of closing the gap between effective and statutory retirement age. Denmark has abolished the possibilities for new entries into early retirement at age 50 to 59, but has kept the possibility to retire early for those aged 60 to 66. Attempts have also been made to curb early retirement in the Netherlands. Dutch labour market exits are collectively agreed at sectoral level, and wage replacement for early retirees over age 55 is financed by topping up unemployment benefits. Until 1994 such a practice was encouraged by the Government but has since been restricted by the 1996 law on administrative penalties, which makes "voluntary" unemployment unlawful (OECD, 1998a). While in Ireland early retirement for labour market reasons (long unemployment periods) also exists, it is of much less importance than in the other three countries.

Most clearly in the Netherlands, but also in Denmark and Austria, the disability pension system has been used for labour market reasons, and such pensions have served as an alternative to other forms of early retirement. Recent attempts to tighten access (stricter medical checks of disability) have led to more outflows from the system and have (at least temporarily) reduced the number of benefit claimants, for example, in the Netherlands. A sort of experience rating has also been introduced, penalizing those firms which make frequent use of the system. The different possibilities for early exit (e.g. via unemployment, early retirement or invalidity pensions) seem to act – in the absence of job opportunities for the elderly – as functional equivalents for each other. If the inflow into one system is restricted, inflow into the other systems increases, albeit not in a 1:1 relation. In Austria such substitution occurred between different invalidity pension systems (Pichelmann, with Hofer, 1999; OECD, 1998a). In the Netherlands the decrease in invalidity pensions has led to an increase in unemployment for the elderly. Reforms have therefore to take account of the possibilities of substitution between several regimes. As their aim is the maintenance or the take-up of jobs for the elderly, they must also set incentives and give organizational help to make such policies of activating the elderly successful. Austria is experimenting with a bonus-malus system, penalizing firms which dismiss older workers and offering incentives to firms employing them.

Mainly because of the existence of functional equivalents to early retirement and the restricted possibilities for older workers to take up jobs, the discontinuation of schemes which have considerably alleviated supply pressures on the labour market, and are popular among firms and workers, should be accompanied by alternative "activation" offers. Otherwise their abolition will lead to greater poverty and uncertainty at the end of working life, and result in more adjustment rigidity for firms. A careful analysis before major changes in the schemes is also legitimized by the fact that these schemes were overwhelmingly offered to men and their abolition coincides with women becoming potentially and increasingly eligible for such schemes. In any case, cuts in passive benefit schemes have to be balanced by offering real alternatives in order to avoid the potential beneficiaries of these systems becoming unemployed or entering another scheme providing for basic subsistence, which has a degrading status. Incentives and/or active labour market policies should be used to maintain older workers in jobs and to ease access to jobs for older workers. Gradual retirement systems are one of the possible measures to be implemented or extended.

Active labour market policies

Activation of labour market policy is currently the most important reform in European labour markets and is the cornerstone of the European Employment Strategy,[4] which is expected ultimately to lead to an increase in employment rates.

All the countries under review have subscribed to this goal. Reducing the share of passive labour market policies and increasing the share of active policies is very much at the top of the agenda. A new social contract between the unemployed and the labour market administration is about to be established: the terms of this contract are that after a certain time spent drawing unemployment benefits, a regular job or an active labour market measure has to be offered. From that moment on (as a rule before 6 months for youth, and 12 months for adults) benefits are only available in exchange for active participation in work or training. This should be seen both as a right to "activation" and a duty for the unemployed to participate in active labour market policy measures.

Countries differ in terms of both overall spending and their shares of active and passive labour market policies (table 3.17). Denmark spends the most, and

Table 3.17 Labour market policy (LMP) expenditure and activity rates[1]

	Total LMP spending[2]	Active LMP	Passive LMP[2]	Activity rate[3]	Activity rate[3] 1997
Austria	1.81	0.39	1.42	21.5	25
Denmark	6.40	1.88	4.59	29.4	31
Ireland	4.32	1.64	2.68	38.0	41
Netherlands	4.85	1.40	3.45	28.9	31

Notes: [1] Average values for the years 1994–97. [2] In percentage of GDP. [3] Share active in total LMP.
Source: OECD: *Employment Outlook*, 1998.

Austria the least. In general active labour market policy increased as a share of total labour market policy (with some fluctuation), confirming a slight move towards activation, whereby this reflected both a relative decline of passive labour market policy (except the Netherlands) and an absolute increase of active labour market policy (except Denmark).

While the level of active labour market policy in the four countries is generally increasing, the composition of measures within it has changed over time, sometimes dramatically. All countries offer a range of measures which fall either into the category of supply-side measures – such as training for youth and adults – or demand-side measures – such as employment subsidies and temporary (public) job creation schemes. In Denmark, for example, labour market training now represents almost 50 per cent of active labour market policies – largely as a consequence of training leave schemes – while youth measures declined in importance, as did subsidized employment. In Ireland, by contrast, subsidized employment now approaches more than 50 per cent of total active labour market policy expenditure, while training measures and youth measures declined relatively in importance. Also in the Netherlands, subsidized employment increased quite considerably with the introduction of so-called "Melkert jobs" (subsidized public jobs for the long-term unemployed), while labour market training and measures for the disabled declined. In Austria, the composition remained rather stable over time.

Countries with high long-term unemployment (the Netherlands, Ireland) are also those that have recently expanded subsidized employment, which can be seen as an appropriate measure for those hard to place in regular jobs.[5] The other two countries more often use training measures, which might be more appropriate for an unemployed population which experiences shorter spells of unemployment. In Denmark a large proportion of labour market training funds serves the employed. Ireland also runs active training measures for the employed, but Austrian and Dutch public labour market training activities are geared almost exclusively towards the unemployed.

Has an active labour market policy contributed to employment success?

It appears that in the absence of active labour market policies, unemployment would have been considerably higher, especially in Denmark and Ireland, which have the highest active labour market policy enrolment figures.[6] Data on outflows from the unemployment register into active labour market policy measures confirm this: for example, in Denmark in 1994, entries to active labour market policy represented around 30 per cent of outflows from the register; comparative figures for Austria and the Netherlands show a rate of outflow of 10 per cent and 17 per cent, confirming the smaller quantitative importance of active labour market policy in the two countries; and no data were available for Ireland. In Denmark outflows into active labour market policy have increased dramatically since 1994, as shown by the fact that 60 per cent of participants in the leave schemes in 1995 were formerly unemployed. It is, for example, estimated that the total fall in unemployment from 1994 to 1996 is attributable to those enrolled in leave schemes (which, because of their job rotation and training aspects, are considered as active measures) and early retirement schemes (Döhrn et al., 1998). For Denmark at least, labour market policy has been a crucial factor in explaining the decrease in unemployment. The question remains whether this is a sustainable solution, however, as those having left unemployment temporarily for a leave scheme might return to unemployment after their leave period. Recent data (see Madsen, 1999) show that this has so far only been the case for some and that those in leave schemes have either left for employment, have continued training or have otherwise left the labour force.

Table 3.18 shows changes in unemployment, employment and participation in active labour market policy measures between 1994 and 1995 (the only years for which we have consistent data). Several observations can be made: in Austria, where active labour market policy is low and remained almost stable (a slight reduction in the numbers of participants occurred), it evidently made no contribution to reducing unemployment; however, it is

Table 3.18. Changes in unemployment, employment and active labour market policy (ALMP) participation[1]

Country	Unemployment (%)	Employment (%)	ALMP entries[2]
Austria	+0.1	+0.6	0
Denmark	−1.0	+1.7	+0.37
Ireland	−2.0	+4.7	+0.15
Netherlands	−0.2	+2.7	−0.07

Notes: [1] Changes for 1994/95 expressed in percentage of the labour force. [2] In full-time equivalents (correction coefficient 0.37).
Sources: European Commission: *Employment in Europe*, 1997; OECD: *Employment Outlook*, 1998; CEPR database.

striking that an increase in the number of unemployed went together with a reduction in the number of those in demand-side (job creation) labour market policy schemes. However, as later increases in unemployment were accompanied by a rise in the number of those participating in schemes, this could be mere coincidence. Measured in the same way, in Denmark the contribution of active labour market policy measures to the reduction in unemployment between 1994 and 1995 was around 40 per cent. Within the active labour market policy measures, "training for the unemployed and those at risk" has expanded. In Ireland, active labour market policy seems to have marginally contributed to the lowering of unemployment and also to employment growth, as demand-side measures (subsidies and public job-creation schemes) have increased. Even in the Dutch case, some effect on the (small) decrease in unemployment and on employment cannot be precluded, as demand-side measures have experienced a small increase despite an overall limited reduction in the numbers participating in active labour market policy measures.

Another way to measure the impact of active labour market policy is the percentage of the labour force served for a given amount of expenditure on active labour market policy. While the above related to the effect of changes over time, the following is concerned with the overall impact on unemployment. The rates should be read as the estimated gross effect of active labour market policy on unemployment, without taking into account dead-weight and other effects which lower gross results, depending on the magnitude of these effects.

Table 3.19 gives information on the number of unemployed persons entering active labour market policy measures in 1995 per 1 per cent of GDP spent on active labour market policies. Gross rates do not control either for employed participants in labour market policies (they are numerous in Ireland and in Denmark) or for duration of measures, but net rates (stocks) do. Net values are estimates of how much unemployment is avoided per 1 per cent of active labour market policy spending in 1995. If these estimated measures are also correct for those countries for which we do not have effective duration data (Ireland, the Netherlands), then table 3.19 shows two things: first, the overall impact of active labour market policy is significant; and, second, there is a large variation between countries in the effectiveness of active labour market policy spending. Active labour market policy has contributed to the recent improvement of the labour market, particularly in Denmark and Ireland. It has quantitatively less importance in both Austria and the Netherlands, both of which, however, have recently experienced an increase in such policy, as is evident from national sources.[7]

While the question of how much active labour market policy has contributed to employment success can only be partially answered quantitatively, there is considerable evidence that it is indeed one of the important qualitative elements of European employment systems, one which has at least prevented

Table 3.19. Participants in active labour market policies for 1 per cent of GDP, 1995 (as percentage of labour force)

Country	Gross[1] (inflows)	Net[2] (stock)
Austria[3]	4.6	1.66
Denmark	9.8	2.70
Ireland	7.1	2.36
Netherlands	1.8	0.9

Notes: [1]OECD: *Employment Outlook*, 1998. [2]Gross inflows controlled for estimated duration for Ireland, the Netherlands and Denmark on the basis of Danish data, corrected for distribution of measures. Duration multiplier of 0.40 for Denmark but 0.50 for Ireland and the Netherlands (subsidized jobs usually have longer duration than training measures). Effective duration for Austria. In percentage of the labour force for 1 per cent of GDP spending. Only unemployed participants. [3]For Austria data are estimates, as only 0.36 per cent of GDP was spent. Effective spending was 1.97 in Denmark, 1.68 in Ireland and 1.28 in the Netherlands.

Sources: OECD: *Employment Outlook,* 1998, on the basis of data provided by the Austrian Employment Service (AMS) and Madson, 1999; author's calculations.

unemployment from skyrocketing during the years of the employment crisis, while contributing to human resource development.

Most importantly, today any definition of full employment has to take account of active labour market policy, which has become an important element of most employment systems. Its importance will increase in future under the European Employment Strategy, which for the first time has established quantitative targets. If the targets are reached (each unemployed youth must be given an active intervention before the sixth month of unemployment and each adult before the twelfth), long-term unemployment will, it is hoped, be a thing of the past. In the four countries under review an equivalent of between 3 and almost 20 per cent of the labour force flow into such measures each year, and without them unemployment would be considerably higher. While active labour market policy remains a "second best solution" after regular employment, it is apparently a necessary solution in today's labour markets.

This is not to say that all measures perform perfectly: various evaluation results using different evaluation methods (OECD, 1996; Meager, 1998) show that there are sometimes high deadweight, substitution and displacement effects linked to the measures. This suggests that some of the unemployed would have found work also in the absence of measures, some measures lead to the replacement of employed persons by (subsidized) unemployed persons, and some subsidized activities displace unsubsidized activities. Various evaluation studies have shown that active measures are more successful in integrating the unemployed into the regular market if they are "close" to regular business activities (where they prepare for marketable jobs or where private enterprises are involved in implementation). O'Connell and McGinnity (1997) show that schemes which are close to such market activities lead to higher efficiency of programmes, especially for women. Programmes seem also to be more effective if they are targeted to the needs of the unemployed and local conditions (Meager, 1998). The latter requires that instead of broad general programmes, smaller specific programmes need to be designed (see also OECD, 1996). We did not address the issue of equal opportunity in labour market policies, mainly because of a lack of data. Rubery (forthcoming) presents some evidence of under-representation of women in programmes, and even a certain trend in programmes to encourage and reinforce the "development of labour market conditions which have proved disadvantageous to women in the labour market" (ibid., p. 53).

Reforms of implementation structures

In all four countries the Public Employment Service (PES), as the main deliverer of measures, has seen its structures changing quite dramatically in a move towards decentralization and "tripartization", one that has also created scope for private placement. In the Netherlands and Austria the PES was removed from the responsibility of the Ministry of Labour and became tripartite organizations run by the social partners. The change involved also a move towards decentralization to regional levels.

In Ireland, a trend towards more local involvement can be seen in the creation of "local employment services" (LES), which are not under the authority of FAS (the national employment service), but fall within the remit of the Department of Enterprise and Trade. LES are mainly responsible for tackling the problem of the long-term unemployed, and are to collaborate with local FAS offices (Employment Services Offices: EOS) and other actors at the local level. In Denmark, together with an activation approach, responsibilities for designing and implementing active labour market policy were given to tripartite regional labour market councils (local authorities, employers and unions).

There has been some evaluation of the working of the new structures: after only four years of the Dutch PES reorganization, an evaluation report of a committee of independent experts found that the changes introduced had not produced the results expected (Dercksen and de Koning, 1996), and that the social partners had neither interacted efficiently nor sufficiently monitored their decentralized offices, especially at central board (CBA) level. Cooperation between the various actors seems to have been much better in the local offices. The Government was criticized for having too many conflicting roles as partner, supervisor and funder. Consequently, some changes have been proposed to give more planning and control authority to the Ministry. The

Ministry will, however, not participate in the CBA, the State being represented by independent members nominated by the Crown. Local and provincial governments will participate in the regional/local boards (RBA) and the PES should concentrate on those hard to place. Incentives (pay by results) will also be used. Despite an unfavourable evaluation, the role of the social partners has not been fundamentally changed.

There has been no evaluation of the Irish reforms: while some see an overlapping of functions between LES and EOS, the Department of Enterprise and Trade sees LES as an additional element in its effort to curb long-term unemployment, with a clear focus on specific local conditions.

Danish evaluations show that the potential risks of decentralization, such as a clash of interest between national and regional targets, seem to be out-weighed by gains of improved targeting of measures to local conditions and a stronger involvement of the local partners. In Austria it was found that the PES works efficiently under the new organizational framework.

While it is difficult to draw definite conclusions on a reorganization in progress, it appears that, in general, policies have been better adapted to divergent local conditions and that the involvement of the social partners and the municipalities (which have become an important actor in the delivery of active labour market policy) has produced encouraging results. Some problems remain, however: the coordination of tasks between the central and the decentralized units should be enhanced, as well as coordination between the different partners on the local level. Central organizations require information on the dealings of their decentralized units, while decentralized units need clear goals, but enough autonomy. Bottom-up definition of goals, the taking into account of divergent local conditions and needs, and an effective system to monitor goal attainment are some of the conditions for an efficient decentralization of PES services (Auer and Kruppe, 1996). Institutional reforms also need a certain time before they work properly. While it is advisable to install a monitoring process accompanying the reforms, it seems to be counter-productive to enact too many fundamental changes in too short a time. Change and stability should be in some balance in order to produce efficient outcomes.

Private placement activities have also gained some importance, particularly in the form of temporary placement agencies. They have seen continuous development in the Netherlands, where they place an increasing number of people. In order to introduce more security for temporary agency workers, the law on "flexicurity" was adopted in 1998 and came into force in 1999. It offers temporary agency workers the prospect of a permanent contract, if they have worked for their agency for a certain period (two years). Some controversies have developed over the effects of the law: certain agencies were accused of deliberately dismissing agency workers to avoid offering them permanent contracts. However, the effects are not yet clear and cannot yet be evaluated. There are also government plans to privatize much of the remaining public employment service, although the effects of privatizing regular placement activities are far from clear. Will this eventually lead to "creaming" and thus leave the hard-to-place with the public employment service, further tarnishing its effectiveness? In the other three countries no such wide-scale privatization of the "social-partnerized" employment service is envisaged, but private placement is now allowed in all of them. In Denmark, competition between private and public placement seems even to have given a new push to the latter.

Another point often raised is whether it is advisable to integrate benefit payment and placement. The conventional wisdom (see, for example, various OECD country economic surveys) is that such an integration is preferable as it permits a better follow-up of the unemployed, provides them with quicker service (e.g. placement in active measures) and allows better control of job search and fraud. "One-stop shops" integrating all labour market services, such as information, counselling, placement, benefit administration and active labour market programmes, are seen as an efficient answer to the coordination problems that arise between different agencies.

In our sample, all countries except Austria have kept their benefit payment agencies separate from the other functions of the employment service. While there are attempts to better coordinate the services (e.g. in the Netherlands through the introduction of a single personal file for the unemployed, even though he or she is served by different services), the basic distinctions still remain.

It is interesting to note that coverage rates (both insurance and assistance benefits) are higher in the three countries with separate services than in Austria with integrated services.[8] This might be due to other reasons such as the existence of unemployed who are freed from job search obligations (e.g. the elderly), but there may be a contradiction between the "welfare" logic of benefit payment agencies and the "activation" logic of placement services which could work against the trend towards the activation of labour market policy. However, this could be mitigated by integrating the two systems.

Conclusion

Both active and passive labour market policies are important tools to regulate employment and unemployment. Passive schemes have enhanced labour market flexibility for companies, and at the same time provided income security for workers affected by unemployment or early retirement. While some changes in unemployment insurance systems have been undertaken to reduce benefit abuse, the reforms should not go so far as to seriously restrict the flexibility of (small) firms and unduly sanction people who have lost their jobs or cannot find jobs in a rationed job market. Early retirement has provided exit flexibility for firms and allowed workers to enjoy a better status than being unemployed at the end of their working lives. The ageing of the workforce and the high costs of the "easy exit" solution, which can also accompany a loss of experienced "human capital", require new solutions. Cuts in the systems, with the aim of reducing costs, might lead to an increase in unemployment for older workers. Therefore, such cuts should only be implemented if other alternatives (namely jobs for older workers) exist, or if firms are willing to maintain employment relationships with their older work-force. Invalidity pension systems, on the other hand, should not be used for labour market purposes, but only for exits based on health grounds. As systems are substitutive, even the ending of access to early retirement via the invalidity pension system has to be compensated for by other exit possibilities, such as early retirement provisions on labour market grounds in order to avoid rising unemployment among the elderly. New ways of organizing exits (such as partial retirement) and of financing (e.g. via mutual funds into which a percen-tage of wage increases is channelled) should and can be found. Such provisions should result in a new distribution of funding between employers, workers and governments. Income security at the end of working life, before regular retire-ment, is an important element of the European system of social protection.

Unless there is a general and sustained recovery of the labour market, active labour market policy will play a decisive role in any new definition of full employment. In all developed countries a certain percentage of the labour force is continuously in active labour market policy measures. This percentage is bound to increase under the European Employment Strategy. In order not to develop secondary labour markets in which only a margina-lized group of people remains permanently, active labour market policy should be used to offer only temporary assistance for individuals in their transition to and from the regular labour market. Labour market policies have to be screened according to that target, and some, such as leave schemes in Denmark and employment companies (*Stahlstiftungen*) which manage redundant labour in Austria, have produced encouraging results.

The timing of policies is important, as the example of Denmark indicates. The implementation of leave schemes fell in a period of labour market recov-ery. Thus, there were net outflows from the schemes into employment. Such a pro-cyclical intervention of labour market policy seems to be particularly effective for training schemes. However, maintaining an anti-cyclical labour market policy intervention is crucial, as such policies are most needed when the economy enters a recession. While the short-term effectiveness of labour market policy is then lower, it should help maintain employment and income until the next upswing. Thus, it contributes to the long-term effective-ness of the labour market. The problem is the lack of advance information on the nature of an economic crisis and its expected duration.

Along with many other labour market institutions, such as employment protection, unemployment benefits, early retirement, or education and training, active labour market policies provide a sort of buffer zone around the regular labour market, and as such are an indispensable element of the

European socio-economic system. This buffer zone is equivalent to so-called transitional labour markets. These labour markets are a permanent feature of modern employment systems and provide temporary bridges into and out of the regular public or private labour market. These transitions between different labour market statuses have become more frequent during the working life of individuals (see Schmid, 1996; Gazier 1998).

Notes

[1]This should not be misinterpreted as suggesting that the unemployed are passive. It is true that there is some controversy about the distinction between active and passive labour market policies. Some active measures might in fact only provide income replacement without any chance of finding jobs in the regular market, while sometimes passive income replacement schemes with a strict obligation of job search lead to recipients finding jobs. The definition used here is based not on the result of policies but on the regulatory level. It is maintained also because otherwise the notion of "activation" of policies, a major policy issue in the countries under review, not least because of the European Employment Strategy, would become somewhat meaningless.

[2]This is of course different for registered unemployment, and unemployment as measured by surveys. In the latter, the unemployed exhausting their benefit entitlement should still be classified as unemployed, provided they fulfil the ILO criteria of being out of work, available and actively searching for jobs. It is probable, but cannot be proved here, that there is some relation between the benefit system and unemployment as measured by surveys, as those receiving benefits and/or being registered might more easily classify themselves as unemployed than those unable to draw benefits. Relations between surveyed unemployment and registered unemployed are complex, however: in Europe, for example, the older registered unemployed are often exempt from job search and should therefore not be counted as unemployed in surveys. Indeed, labour force survey unemployment is usually lower than registered unemployment.

[3]In Austria, 79.5 per cent of the unemployed held a job before becoming unemployed. Comparative figures are 63.5 per cent for Denmark, 53.8 per cent for the Netherlands and only 25.7 per cent for Ireland. There are marked differences in these figures for men and women: Austria, men: 90 per cent; women: 65.5 per cent; Denmark, men: 68.3 per cent; women: 59.7 per cent; Ireland, men: 30.6 per cent; women: 18 per cent; the Netherlands, men: 54.1 per cent; women: 53.6 per cent.

[4]The European Employment Strategy has been gradually developed since the publication in 1993 of the *White Paper on growth, competitiveness and employment* through many European Council resolutions. Employment was finally integrated as a title in the Amsterdam Treaty of 1997. The Extraordinary Job Summit in Luxembourg at the end of 1997 laid the basis for the implementation of the strategy. The Commission enacts guidelines, which are implemented and monitored by the member States through National Action Plans. Four policy areas are covered: employability, entrepreneurship, adaptability and equal opportunities.

[5]There seems also to be some relation between youth unemployment and the share of youth measures within a country: countries with high youth unemployment (Denmark, Ireland) usually spend a larger share of active labour market policy expenditure on youth than those with low youth unemployment (Austria). An exception is the Netherlands: until recently high youth unemployment went hand in hand with low relative spending.

[6]Our figures are as follows: for example, for Denmark gross effects for certain years are estimated on the basis of entries and duration of measures. In estimated gross terms, around 200,000 people (full-time equivalents) out of 550,000 participated in active labour market policy measures in 1995. Of these, an estimated 95,000 were already employed participants in labour market training. A first gross estimate then shows that unemployment would have been 105,000 higher without measures, i.e. the unemployment rate would have been roughly 11 per cent instead of 7.2 per cent in 1995. For the other countries, similar estimates result in unemployment reduction rates of 3.3 percentage points for Ireland, 0.7 for Austria and 1.0 for the Netherlands.

[7]In Austria, inflows into measures almost doubled between 1993 and 1997, reaching 112,280 people in 1997, corresponding to an annual average of around 38,000 people (about 2.9 per cent of

the labour force in flow and 1 per cent in stock terms). The Netherlands has also increased its active labour market policy: however, the most important current measure with regard to participants is a labour tax cut for those employed on low wages, with some 780,000 participants in 1996. Specific jobs in the public sector for the long-term unemployed (the so-called Melkert jobs) have also been created. Interestingly, spending has not increased, which might indicate that the tax cut is not included in the spending figures.

[8] In 1995 these coverage rates were 149 per cent in Ireland, 127 per cent in the Netherlands, 100 per cent in Denmark and 90 per cent in Austria (OECD, 1997). Coverage rates are defined as the number of registered unemployed receiving benefits with respect to the number of unemployed according to the labour force survey (LFS) definition. Other definitions (e.g. benefit receivers among LFS/ILO defined unemployed) show, however, much lower figures: Ireland 82 per cent, Austria 74.6 per cent, Denmark 68.2 per cent, Netherlands 62.2 per cent (Rubery, forthcoming).

GENERAL CONCLUSIONS

4

RELATIVE SUCCESS CONFIRMED BY RECENT DATA

In Chapter 1 of this report, we presented an overview of the different dimensions of labour market success and the problems still to be tackled. We found that countries have indeed succeeded in reducing unemployment to low (or at least lower) levels, and that this reduction in unemployment has accelerated over recent years in three of the countries under review. We also discovered that employment has risen, employment rates have increased and gender gaps have at least quantitatively been reduced.

Table 4.1 confirms the conclusions drawn in Chapter 1 for the most recent period: the countries under review have continued to reduce unemployment to low(er) levels, or to maintain it at low levels. In addition, some of the countries have recently seen a rapid increase in employment and in employment rates. In most cases, gender gaps have been reduced, but remain considerable, especially in full-time equivalents (taking into account working time). Youth unemployment has also continued to decline, as has long-term unemployment.

This success is particularly visible when the four countries are compared to some of the bigger countries in Europe, such as Germany, France and Italy, which still suffer from depressed labour markets with very high levels of overall unemployment, and youth and long-term unemployment.[1] While unemployment in Ireland has declined rapidly, it is still high compared with the three other countries. However, it has fallen below the EU average. Ireland is also experiencing a fast decline in youth and long-term unemployment, albeit from a high level. Even Austria, which had maintained low levels of unemployment over a long period, but had lately seen a small increase, has most recently achieved a small decrease. In addition, it has both low youth and long-term unemployment.

Both Denmark and the Netherlands now have very low levels of open unemployment. Since 1998, both have been among the EU countries with

Table 4.1. Relative labour market success: Recent data

Country	ER (1998)	FT ER (1998)	EMP (1994-98)	UR[1] (July 1999)	LTU (1998)	YUR[1] (July 1999)	YUG[1] (July 1999)	Gender gaps				
								ER	FT ER	UR (July 1999)	LTU (1998)	YUR (July 1999)
Austria	70.1	65.0	0.0	4.3	1.6	5.7	1.4	21.1	28.7	1.5	0.3	2.4
Denmark	79.2	69.9	1.8	4.5	1.4	6.9	2.4	12.7	22.1	1.9	1.0	-0.1
Ireland[2]	60.5	56.5	5.0	6.7	5.7	9.0	2.3	26.1	38.9	0.1	1.8	-0.1
Netherlands	68.3	54.0	2.3	3.2	1.9	7.2	4.0	23.8	37.8	2.8	0.8	7.6
France	60.8	57.4	-0.7	11.0	5.1	25.1	14.1	14.7	24.5	3.8	1.6	4.1
Germany	61.5	55.2	-0.7	9.1	5.0	9.0	0.1	15.7	26.9	1.4	1.2	-1.5
Italy	51.8	50.2	-0.2	12.0	8.4	32.0	20.0	29.2	35.2	7.7	4.9	10.2
United Kingdom	71.4	60.9	1.2	6.1	2.0	13.1	7.0	14.4	32.6	1.6	-1.3	-3.7
EU[3]	61.0	55.0	n.a.	9.3	4.9	17.8	8.5	20.0	26.1	3.2	1.7	3.4
United States[4]	75.9	n.a.	1.80	4.3	n.a.	9.9	5.6	13.8	n.a.	0.4	n.a.	-1.3

Notes: ER: Employment rate. FTER: Full-time equivalent employment rate. EMP: Employment growth, 1992–97. UR: Unemployment rate. LTU: Long-term unemployment rate. YUR: Youth unemployment rate. YUG: Youth gap (difference between total UR and YUR). Gender gaps: difference between male and female values. [1] Netherlands: June 1999; Italy: April 1999; Denmark: June 1999; United Kingdom: May 1999. [2] LTU: 1997 data. [3] Gender gaps for ER, FT ER and LTU: 1997 data. [4] EMP: 1992–97 data.

Sources: European Commission: *Joint Employment Report*, 1999; OECD: *Labour Force Statistics*, 1999; Eurostat, News Release 90/99.

the lowest unemployment rates and have surpassed Austria in that regard. Denmark has also by far the highest employment rates (both in gross and in full-time equivalent rates). It is also the country with the smallest gender gap in employment rates. On the contrary, the Netherlands has comparatively low employment rates in full-time equivalents, because of the importance of part time work. This is also the reason for high gender gaps in full-time equivalent rates, as women work overwhelmingly part time.

Even if Dutch unemployment levels come close to the traditional definition of full employment (3 per cent), none of the countries has yet reached full employment if qualitative criteria are also included. There is some way to go before we can speak of absolute and not relative success. However, while this employment success has been accompanied by a change in the structure of employment from permanent full-time jobs to a more heterogeneous pattern of work (such as part-time and temporary jobs), it seems not to have been at the price of a general fall in real wages and a sharp rise in inequalities. Although the latter question has not been analysed exhaustively, and there seem to be considerable differences between the four countries (e.g. inequalities seem to have risen more in Ireland, and also in the Netherlands, than in Denmark and Austria – see Annex I), the overall conclusion is that at least three of the countries, which belong to the Northern and Central European socio-economic model, produce fewer inequalities than those which are based on a free market approach such as the United States and the United Kingdom. This results from collective bargaining between the social partners within systems of "corporatist governance" but is also due to the efficiency of the social transfer system in reducing poverty . While the social transfer system has been much criticized for inefficiently allocating public money, such criticism has certainly been blunted by the recent changes introduced in the system, especially the "activating" elements in labour market policies. This will make it increasingly more difficult to draw "passive" benefits for long periods.

SOME ELEMENTS FROM THE ANALYSIS OF SUCCESS

This book selected macroeconomic policy, social dialogue and labour market policy (including labour market reforms) for an explanation of the relative success in the labour markets of the four countries. The interplay of these three dimensions seems to have been decisive for labour market recovery. We also showed briefly how gender and working-time policies have transformed the labour markets of the four countries, resulting in more heterogeneity, and discussed the contribution of education and training.

Below we consider these and other factors which seem to be behind the relative success of the four countries. We have divided these factors into those which are common to all countries and those which are particular to one country.

COMMON FACTORS

Table 4.2 shows some of the common and specific factors which explain part of the success. While all countries differ in many important details even in those common factors, three such factors of success have been found.

The first is corporatist governance and social dialogue, combining mutual information and discussion of issues at higher levels with the ability to implement reforms on lower levels. This is turn facilitates wage moderation and is conducive to policy-making, combining the divergent interests of specific groups with the interests of society and the economy as a whole.

Three of the countries have reinvigorated social dialogue, after experiencing economic hardship and high unemployment rates in the beginning of the 1980s. The dialogue has contributed to creating a climate of confidence between the social partners, and moderate wage policy has accommodated a stabilization-oriented macroeconomic policy. But the social partners have also been engaged in reforms of social security, the labour market and labour market policy.

These reforms have not always been easy for the partners, especially trade unions, to accept. The latter have made concessions in order to reinvigorate the economy, and have agreed to changes which have not always been in the short-term interests of their members. That these changes (e.g. in social security administration and social transfer benefit levels), which were combined with moderate wage increases, have not been accompanied by social unrest is certainly one of the achievements of social dialogue.

It has been found that institutions that permit communication at high levels are of particular importance when conducting social dialogue, while it is imperative also to have a dialogue at lower levels and not only between the organizations, but also within them. For example, the adherence of the

Table 4.2. Overview: Factors of success in the labour market

Austria	Strong and steady corporatist governance; coordinated macroeconomic policy; traditionally strong role of government sector; temporary fiscal expansion on a general background of fiscal consolidation; wage moderation; tax reforms; high labour market flexibility; labour supply reduction policies; lay-off system; (apprenticeship) training.
Denmark	Renewed corporatist governance; coordinated macroeconomic policy; strong role of government sector; temporary fiscal expansion on the background of fiscal consolidation; tax reforms; wage moderation; labour market policy (leave schemes, activation, early retirement) and a lay-off system; labour market reform; (continuous) training; labour supply reduction.
Ireland	Increasing corporatist governance and macroeconomic coordination; fiscal consolidation; wage moderation; tax reforms; foreign direct investment; European Structural Fund; active labour market policy; (university) training.
Netherlands	Renewed corporatist governance; coordinated macroeconomic policy and fiscal consolidation; welfare reform; tax reforms; working time; labour market reforms; labour supply reduction.

rank-and-file members to policies agreed by top representatives is essential for policy success.

The second factor is a macroeconomic policy oriented primarily towards price, interest and exchange rate stability, but also – in a limited but sometimes significant manner – providing fiscal stimuli to the economy against a general background of fiscal consolidation. What looks at first sight to be a contradiction in terms must not be so. It seems that, having reduced their deficits, countries are recovering some of their abilities to intervene anti-cyclically in the economy and this is certainly one of the beneficial effects of the EMU. But unlike in the 1970s, when such spending went out of control, today governments seem to be able to use the beneficial short-term effects of fiscal expansion, but then revert to fiscal consolidation in the next round. In all countries, but in particular in Austria and Denmark, government expenditure has been important although it declined as a share in GDP. Without government expenditure, growth would have been much lower. The question is, however, whether governments spend money efficiently and if lower spending leading to lower taxes would have even been more beneficial for the economy. There are arguments in favour of a "crowding out" of private by public spending, but our study has not found evidence of this.

Therefore we consider government spending and private activities to be mutually supportive, and while fiscal consolidation is to be pursued, the claims that "lean" government is the answer to all problems in the labour market cannot be supported for the European welfare economies. Fiscal expansion within some margins is important when the economy is entering a recession, and fiscal consolidation should be used to re-establish the possibility of governments to intervene anti-cyclically in the economy, when there is a need for it. This is compatible with the criteria established for the EMU. Having some room to manoeuvre in fiscal policy is especially crucial, as there is virtually no scope for national monetary policies under the EMU. (See also the conclusions of the country reviews of the International Monetary Fund, for example, for Austria and the Netherlands – IMF, 1998). However, concerted efforts are also required to establish a European monetary policy which, while being stability oriented, accommodates such an anti-cyclical fiscal policy.

Nor does this preclude further reduction of the structural components of government budgets, especially government debt servicing. In general, we need more research on the different employment intensities of the various forms of government spending, which could be used to propose shifts in spending. However, investments have already been singled out as such an employment-intensive expenditure.

Third, labour market policy (both active and passive) and labour market reforms have had an impact on the recovery of the labour markets. Labour market policy has to be seen in the context of labour market regulations: especially passive, income-replacement schemes, but also active labour market policy measures such as labour market training are instruments which provide both security for workers and adjustment flexibility for firms. Without such a buffer, firms would have to bear the brunt of the costs and the social consequences of adjustment, and workers would face high insecurity. Our study has clearly shown that labour market policy is one of the pillars of the European Welfare States. While this conclusion does not preclude the necessity for further reforms, for example, to activate measures in order to prevent the rise of long-term unemployment, policy-makers should be aware of the basic function of labour market policy and its interrelation with employment protection and the general functioning of labour markets. Reforms in the delivery of labour market policies (e.g. through employment services) have also contributed to the success of the countries, by making policies more responsive to local and company needs.

In particular, the policy of activating labour market policy has already shown its positive impact. This policy corresponds to a new implicit contract between benefit recipients and the different benefit administrations, with a new stress on rights and duties.

COUNTRY-SPECIFIC FACTORS

Country-specific factors of success include, for example, Ireland's success in attracting foreign direct investment (helped by low corporate tax rates) and support from the European structural funds. Together these factors have helped to raise Irish GDP, but means that Ireland will in the future lose the special support of the structural funds and has probably to prepare for lower growth rates.

For the Netherlands, such factors include a successful policy of part-time work which eased the labour market integration of women. The high percentage of voluntary part-time work shows that much of it corresponds to the preferences of the workforce. This goes with substantial temporary agency activity, which has also contributed to labour market mobility. A policy of "flexicurity", which tries to combine the flexibility of temporary work with some of the security of permanent positions, and welfare reform accommodating flexible jobs could avoid the danger of developing a large sector of "precarious" work. In the Netherlands, through flexible working time, supply and demand have been better matched than in some of the other countries.

Moreover, the country has also ingeniously reformed its Welfare State. Such reforms are an important pillar of the "Polder model". The general trend is not the simple abolition of the Welfare State, but a new distribution of responsibilities. The Government sets (and sometimes controls) the rules, such as benefit levels, but policy administration is mandated to the social partners or private companies and organizations. The users of the systems (companies and their workers) have to contribute more than before to the social protection system (e.g. through experience rating). This encourages actors to behave "responsibly". Companies should be interested in preventing risks (such as bad health) and should not easily permit the exit of elderly workers to the invalidity pension scheme, which is now more costly to them. It seems that the Dutch reforms are an example of how the social protection system can indeed be made more "productive", but a thorough evaluation of the new way of running the system is still required. There might well be major drawbacks for some as a result of these policies: for example, recent conflicts in the dockyards showed that the privatization of the pension system had led to large pension reductions for workers (EIRO news).

One factor ensuring flexibility in Austria is the strong reaction of labour supply to business cycle changes. This also concerns the large seasonal sector of the economy and the corresponding reactivity of, in particular, the foreign workforce, but also youths' and women's supply behaviour reacting to business cycle changes. Despite the high degree of labour market regulation, both employment and unemployment flows are dynamic and the labour market shows a high labour turnover, supported by the unemployment benefit system. Austria has also successfully achieved the privatization of its nationalized industries, accompanied by specific labour force adjustment programmes which have dampened privatization's impact on the labour market. The apprenticeship system has also been a factor in explaining low youth unemployment. Recently, reforms have been undertaken which have removed some of the disincentives (e.g. high marginal taxes) to take up work. Labour market policy is also on the increase.

A lay-off system supports labour market flexibility in Denmark. But in addition, Denmark is an example of the activation strategy initiated by the EU, and its good results, for example, in curbing youth unemployment are linked to this strategy. The strategy introduces new rights and new obligations for the unemployed: the drawing of passive benefits over a longer period is no longer possible, especially for young people, who have to accept activation offers instead, if they do not want to lose their benefits. Leave schemes, which increase labour market flexibility (while maintaining security in not breaking the link to the labour market) through job rotation are another important explanation for Danish labour market success. Denmark has also most consistently had recourse to temporary fiscal expansion to stimulate the economy and has used the fruits of expansion to revert to fiscal consolidation thereafter.

THE EFFICIENT COMBINATION OF POLICIES AND INSTITUTIONS

More than from isolated policy actions, labour market success seems to result from an efficient combination of factors. Our study offers some indications on how such interactions might work. At the macroeconomic level, tight monetary policy, fiscal consolidation and wage moderation policies seem to have accommodated each other. Austria is a good example of how to introduce long-term stability by such a coordination of policies.

More specifically, in the labour markets in Denmark and Austria, weak dismissal protection (on the regulation side in Denmark and de facto in Austria) seems to go together with relatively strong (income) protection at the societal level (whereby unemployment benefits are higher in Denmark than in Austria). In these countries, where small and medium-sized firms prevail, such systems seem to support the economy and the labour market and add to flexibility, resulting in low shares of long-term unemployment. These countries also have high employment rates. For small firms and the seasonal sector and its workforce, this arrangement seems to be a stabilizing factor, although it does involve some cross-subsidization. As can be seen from Austria, this does not preclude the extension of flexible working time to cope with some strong seasonal fluctuations.

Other such efficient combinations include the temporary demand injection in the economy combined with a training-based job rotation scheme in Denmark, or the combination of part-time work, a basic pension scheme and placement activities of temporary work agencies in the Netherlands.

In general, systemic elements working in the same direction are more efficient than elements working in opposite directions. If systemic elements in employment systems are congruent, employment performance is better. The Danish employment system might be taken as an example of how such elements interact: high labour turnover is supported not only by the lay-off system, but also by labour market training, which itself is congruent with training leave schemes. Denmark also has both parental leave schemes and childcare provisions which allow more possibilities for women to participate in working life.

A combination of policies, which results in both flexibility for firms and security for workers, might be the most appropriate institutional arrangements in European labour markets. To varying degrees, at least three of the four countries have managed to set up such arrangements.

However, given the complexity of these systems, thorough research is needed to determine the precise effect of such combinations. Timing is also important: temporary leave schemes might be efficient bridges to the regular labour market in an upswing, but possibly not in a downturn, as most of the leavers will probably once again be unemployed after their leave. In an unpredictable and complex world, such combinations and the right timing also need some luck in order to add up to successful policies.

DO SMALL COUNTRIES HAVE SPECIFIC ADVANTAGES?

The countries under review are small: only the Netherlands can be considered medium-sized. The four countries account for around 10 per cent of the European Union's GDP and 9 per cent of its total labour force (table 4.3).

Table 4.3. GDP and labour force (LF) as a percentage of total EU, 1996

Austria		Denmark		Ireland		Netherlands	
GDP	LF	GDP	LF	GDP	LF	GDP	LF
2.44	2.28	2.00	1.67	0.90	0.88	4.43	4.44

Source: ILO CEPR data bank.

While the three factors of a sound macroeconomic environment and policy, social dialogue and labour market policy might produce their effects also in bigger countries, the small size of the countries under review might be an additional factor in their success. Katzenstein (1985) has outlined some of the factors, which distinguish small from larger developed countries. The first is economic openness, which is in part due to the small size of domestic markets: "Dependence on imports and the necessity to export make the economies of the small European States both more open and more specialized than those of larger countries" (ibid, p. 87). Second comes democratic corporatism based on an ideology of social partnership, a system of centralized and concentrated interest groups, and voluntary and informal coordination of conflicting objectives. However, while there might be some other advantage in being small, such as a more homogeneous labour force and better governability (and thus better cooperation between actors), this alone cannot be an important factor as most of the countries went through a major crisis before their present recovery. It could be, however, that once a successful system of "corporatist governance" is established or reinvigorated, smallness becomes again a distinct advantage, because of the smaller "power elite" circles. This in turn leads to more informality and closer personal relationships, which are an important condition for successful bargaining and consensus.

This aspect is certainly one of the reasons for the success of the Austrian system of social partnership. The system was run in the 1970s by powerful leaders on both sides, who have since given way to a somewhat more depersonalized style of governance. Not least because of the danger of such systems becoming top-heavy, there must be a continuous connection with their constituents, in order to ensure adequate interest representation. The skill of governance in democratic corporatist systems is to represent group interests and match them with the interests of the larger economy. This is not always easy. For example, the latest bargaining round in Denmark was ended by government intervention because the union bargainers did not have the support of their rank and file.

What can other countries learn from small countries?

It is not only smallness which is important here, but the traditions and cultures which form the background to different institutions, and which might make it harder to understand and transfer experience from one country to another. In particular, it might be very difficult to adapt "democratic corporatism" in countries with a liberal, pluralist tradition of policy formulation.

However, smaller countries can teach bigger countries at least two lessons. First, while "democratic corporatism" per se is not the answer to all labour market problems, it seems that once a real dialogue is established within the overall framework of corporatism, solutions to the problems can be found. This also shows that problems are never purely economic but have always a political dimension, which relates to the forms of governance. And corporatism seems to be a form of governance which is equally efficient in running the economy as liberal pluralist (market-led) forms of governance. Particularly if equity issues are taken into account, corporatist governance has clearly superior performance (see Annex I). The problem of corporatist governance countries was up to now their failing employment performance. With this problem solved, the countries seem to have developed into successful socio-economic models.

The second lesson is that economic openness pays off and that there seem to be no longer-term negative effects of globalization on the labour markets of developed countries, or at least no such problems which remain unsolved. As well as these two major elements (form of governance and degree of economic openness), there are many other examples of policy elements from the four success cases, which might help some of the larger European countries overcome their labour market problems. For example, there is no reason why bigger countries should not be able to introduce job-rotation schemes along Danish lines or part-time regulations like the Dutch. A job-rotation system (adapted from the Danish model) was, for example, recently introduced in Austria, which has rather similar institutions to Germany. Concerning part-time work, in particular, equal treatment with full-time work is important. There could also be advantages in introducing a three-pillar financing system for retirement (a basic pension, a contribution-based system and a private top-up), as in Denmark or in the Netherlands, in other countries as well. And the Austrian (and German) apprenticeship system may well still serve as a model for the introduction of alternative training in other countries. These are only some examples of many which show that it is not impossible to transfer elements of one system to another. It is almost certain that such convergence of policies and regulations will be stimulated by the EMU, which will inevitably lead to more adjustment in various policy fields.

Another of these "convergence drivers" is the European Employment Strategy. The common guidelines and the associated monitoring process must be expected to lead to more convergence in employment and labour market policies. While it will render labour market policy more active, it should also be considered that there might be limits to a total activation of the labour market, and that there are justified passive elements in the social protection system as well, especially in old age and for single parents.

We will refrain from a discussion of the transferability of elements of the small European cases to countries outside the realm of the core developed countries. This problem cannot be addressed without a thorough analysis of the institutional and economic conditions in these other countries (e.g. transition countries or developing countries). Concerning the form of governance, "democratic corporatism" could serve as a model for governance, but the political prerequisites (e.g. strong and equal partners) are usually not met. However, even grass-roots corporatism at local level could be developed later into a more centralized form of democratic corporatism. In any case, there seems to be no real alternative to a dialogue between social actors in order to have some governability in the economy, and this basic principle could apply worldwide.

Is success sustainable?

Richard Freeman, during the 1997 assembly of the European Association of Labour Economists, spoke of the "war of the models" and saw increasing heterogeneity in the world economy and the coexistence of (and competition between) many socio-economic models. All four countries are sometimes presented as distinctive models, the most prominent being the Dutch "Polder" model. However, the Irish "Celtic Tiger" model, the Austrian "Danube" model – a variant of the "Rhineland" model – and the Danish "Viking" model also have their strengths. Yet we do not propose that such entire models, which have developed within specific national traditions, institutions and policies, should be copied by other countries. This is not only because such a transplant is impossible but also because many of the models that have hitherto been proposed as best-practice examples have in the meantime lost much of their glitter (e.g. the Japanese, the Swedish or the "Asian Tiger" model). Even without proposing the transplantation of these models, discussion of the "lessons" learned from the analysis of the four small countries requires a look at the question of the sustainability of (relative) success.

Continued success will of course be facilitated when the three factors relevant for success – social dialogue, stability-oriented macroeconomic policy and labour market policy, including labour market reform – are maintained. For example, for all countries, we have identified the ability to conduct a social dialogue as one of the factors in success, and a big threat to all four countries is a return to more adversarial practices, which had in the past been responsible for labour market problems. In some of the countries unions are now claiming a bigger share of the cake after some years of wage restraint, which saw profits and stock markets soaring. Particularly with declining unemployment, first signs of labour shortages are developing, which make it more difficult to maintain a restrictive wage policy. Employers instead ask for even more restraint and more deregulation, especially in wages.

New items on the bargaining agenda, especially those dealing with workforce ageing such as restrictions on early retirement provisions and pension reforms, might develop into conflicts. Recent conflicts show that social dialogue can be fragile even in countries which have a deep-rooted system of "corporatist governance" (e.g. Denmark). Maintenance of social dialogue and the will to find compromises which will not alienate one of the parties are therefore the best guarantee for continued success.

Stability-oriented macroeconomic policy has been a pillar of success and while it might now become marginally less tight, a return to outright deficit spending will not result in sustained success in labour markets. The policy of activating labour market policy should also be continued, as it has shown its effectiveness. It should, however, react to labour shortages (no active measures – except training – are needed in areas of workforce shortages) and also maintain some of the passive policies which have resulted in labour market success in the past.

Besides these three major points, sustainability of success also depends on how the countries will cope with new challenges. Very briefly, some of these selected challenges are:

- *Ireland*: the reduction of EU structural funds investments to Ireland, and even more importantly a possible crisis in the computer industry. While Ireland has a competitive advantage in this growth sector, it also remains vulnerable if its domestic industry and services cannot compensate for a possible slowdown in the sector.

- *Austria*: the country will have to cope with the gradual opening of the EU to its low-wage Eastern neighbours. How it deals with this problem will in part determine to what extent it remains successful in the labour market. This is also an industrial relations problems, as Austrian employers are less reluctant than unions to open the borders to cheap labour.

- *The Netherlands*: further success will also depend on the development of women's employment participation. Will they continuously opt for part-time work or increasingly ask for full-time jobs (a development which has been seen in the Scandinavian countries), and is the economy able to provide them with these jobs?

- *Denmark*: labour market policy expenditures are at a high level and activation of policies has been pursued more consistently than in many other countries. If a recession comes, will Denmark still be able to use labour market policies in an appropriate way?

IS FULL EMPLOYMENT STILL POSSIBLE TODAY?

Three of the four countries are already near the traditional "full-employment" unemployment rate of 3 per cent. However, analysis of their labour markets reveals that the old notion of full employment, i.e. full-time labour force participation from age 15 to 65, has become rather meaningless. The transformations in European employment systems in the last 30 years have been considerable: generally, they have seen a decline in male employment and an increase in female employment. In purely quantitative terms, women have been the "winners" in employment creation during these years, while men have been the losers. This development was accompanied by a shift from agriculture and the industrial sector to the service sector. In a certain way, older industrial male workers even shifted to a new, fourth sector, the "inactive leisure-redundancy sector" to which early retirees and – given longer life expectancy – those retiring at the standard age belong. Through reductions in working time, most of the employed have also enjoyed more leisure than at any time before. However, there is also a considerable share of people who were forced into this "leisure–redundancy" sector, namely the long-term unemployed and all those who left the labour market with less than generous redundancy packages.

In the active segment of the labour market, this shift went together with a change in types of employment. While the permanent, full-time employment relationship is still dominant, at least for men, so-called "atypical" forms of work are on the increase. Part-time work, sometimes with just a few hours of weekly working time, fixed-term contracts, temporary agency work, work on call and telework, as well as a rise in non-agricultural self-employment and a diversity of working-time patterns, have brought a new heterogeneity to the world of work. Women, in particular, often work part time, and this is frequently combined with temporary work as well. In addition, the number of participants in active labour market measures (or other temporary situations, which have supply-reducing – and possibly enhancing – effects, such as internships) has multiplied; the former is also being increased by the implementation of the European Employment Strategy.

Should all forms be considered equally as work and enter into a new definition of full-time work, or should only full-time (and part-time) "regular" permanent work – which is still by far the dominant element in the labour market – be considered "decent" work? Here the second ILO criteria for the definition of full-time work – that such work should be freely chosen – is helpful. "Freely chosen" is sometimes hard to determine, given the constraints of everyday life, such as the general need to earn a (double) income to face living costs, or to work part time because of the difficulties of integrating working life with family responsibilities.

Freely chosen part-time work should of course be part of the new definition, as should all forms of work which correspond to changes in the supply side of the labour market and new preferences of the population. An additional criterion could be that all forms of work, which act (or at least are intended to act) as bridges into the labour market (this is more often than not true of temporary work) could be included. Participation in "activation" measures, in which it becomes more common to link the right to benefits with a duty to be "activated", would fall into the latter category. That is to say, any new notion of full employment has to be based on flow aspects of the labour market and not just stocks. Full employment should reflect the new heterogeneity of working life to a certain extent, but participation in full-time permanent work must be an option for everyone at certain points in an individual's career. However, the new heterogeneity of the labour market also demands the reform of social security and employment protection which should extend beyond individual firms, and ensure employment and the employability of individuals as well as their income.

Compared to the situation 30 years ago, supply has shrunk at both the entry and the exit sides of the labour market through more comprehensive and longer education, and through earlier retirement. Without this supply reduction, unemployment would probably be much higher today, given the "lean employment" environment of the competitive firm. So, under the condition of a reduced supply and the inclusion of some "atypical" but freely chosen forms of work, and participants in labour market measures "in transition" to the regular labour market, full employment is still possible. To put it in a nutshell: while the regular public or private labour market (including dependent employed and self-employed) should remain the main destination, many of the "transitional labour market statuses", such as education and work, work and retirement, socially useful work, active labour market measures, and so on – which can be seen as "buffer zones" around the regular labour market – should be included in a new notion of full employment.

If this is not the case, and only full-time equivalent work is considered "full employment", there is a long way to go, and there might even be no road leading towards this ambitious aim. The goal should be situated somewhere between a pure quantitative consideration, as expressed by non-adjusted employment rates, and the full-time equivalent employment rates, which set such a full-time definition as the target. Measured according to this target, some of the recent employment "success stories" have a poor record, owing to the growth of non-standard employment. However, large parts of this are voluntary and add up to new ways of combining family with working life.

Besides activation strategies, room should also be left for "passive" income-replacement schemes. We have shown that unemployment benefit schemes sometimes act as a well-functioning "flexicurity" device in certain sectors of the labour market that practise a lay-off system. While an increase in effective retirement age is desirable, matching statutory and effective age will be a difficult task as firms are reluctant to retain older workers. This is shown by the fact that older workers are generally the category best protected by dismissal regulations, but are usually a priority target of redundancies. A conclusion is that some of the early retirement schemes should be maintained, while more effort has to be made to ensure that firms retain their older workers, at least on a part-time basis in partial retirement schemes. Different financing instruments have to be found (such as allocating a proportion of wage increases to collectively bargained funds), while support for changes in work organization, training adapted to the needs of the older workforce and possibly wage subsidies, could be part of a set of incentives for employers to retain older workers.

All this has serious implications for the notion of full employment, and also for the recently adopted notion of decent work in the ILO Director-General's report to the International Labour Conference (ILO, 1999). While decent work basically tries to link the quantity and the quality aspect of employment and concerns foremost the creation of greater employment and income opportunities for as many people as possible, it also includes the "employment environment" of social protection. It recognizes the need for security and protection without denying that flexibility of adaptation for firms is needed too. This naturally places security not only within companies and the public sector, but also beyond firms and administrations. The catchword of "employability" underlines this need quite clearly. Therefore the notion of full employment has to be extended to include "employability" and should be seen more in a flow perspective of individuals to whom lifetime employability is assured. This implies that the status of someone employable is transformed into the status of employed, and that periods of *intermittent* employability see some form of income and social protection as well as meaningful activity such as training. Such a new notion of full employment needs of course a thorough discussion throughout the ILO and its constituents, before it can be translated into substantive regulations, such as new international labour Conventions.

Note

[1]With the difference that Germany has both low youth and gender gaps, while youth and gender gaps are considerable in France and Italy.

POLICY RECOMMENDATIONS

5

1. Social dialogue

In increasingly complex societies, a continuous dialogue on important matters concerning the welfare of nations and citizens is imperative. Through such "social concertation" divergent views of the world (due to the divergent interests of constituents) can be voiced and compromises found. Therefore institutions of social dialogue should be reinvigorated or established in order to ensure that a continuous exchange is maintained even in the countries which are among the world leaders in social dialogue. Austria is a good example of how a long-term continuous dialogue has contributed to stability and, despite current difficulties, a basically healthy labour market. As far as the institutions permitting such a dialogue are concerned, the Netherlands Economic and Social Council and the Labour Foundation can serve as models. They integrate the dialogue with research and advice, and ensure its continuity. Such continuity is of great importance, as the dialogue is fragile, as can be seen by frequent government intervention in some of the countries. Such direct intervention (e.g. in bargaining) should be prevented by the dialogue. The countries should therefore strive to have "social concertation" institutionalized at a high level. These dialogue institutions should preferably also have secretariats, including analysis units.

It is vital that participation in such a dialogue is not limited to high levels only, but that it is also established or maintained at lower (sectoral or regional) levels. It has also to be ensured that the "rank and file" of representative organizations are duly informed of policy processes at higher levels in order to avoid conflicts and facilitate the implementation of agreements. The dialogue might at times be bipartite, but given the importance of government in all four countries, it has to be tripartite in matters of common concern. It should also take account of the fact that organizations other than trade unions and employers might represent people's interests (e.g. non-governmental organizations).

At present, social dialogue has come under pressure from many sides: after years of restraint, workers are asking for a larger share of the cake, employers are often unhappy with the slow decision process in the system, and many conflicts surround the introduction of new items on the bargaining agenda such as employment maintenance and early retirement issues. But there is no other way to solve these problems except by an ongoing dialogue. Social dialogue has been a powerful condition for success, and from this it follows that its disintegration would be an equally powerful reason for the countries to return to the crisis years, with adverse effects for all their citizens.

2. Macroeconomic policy

There is no doubt that the stabilization policies pursued at the macro level have had positive effects. It seems that a rather tight monetary policy and quasi-fixed exchange rates have already preceded the EMU and have been beneficial for the economy in the long run. Monetary policy might in certain phases (e.g. at the time of German reunification) have been more accommodating. With very low inflation, there is some room for a somewhat less restrictive monetary policy at the European level. However, decisions on monetary policy no longer lie in the hands of the governments of the four countries. From this stems also a need for consensus building, cooperation and coordination of monetary policies (and macroeconomic policies in general) on the European level. Not only stability, but also growth and employment, should be goals of European monetary policy.

There is also some room for manoeuvre in fiscal policies. While here, too, consolidation policies have been proved correct, consolidation should aim once more to allow anti-cyclical intervention if the need arises.

Government expenditure should be screened according to the different employment intensities of budget elements (while also observing equity issues); given the small scope for fiscal intervention, governments could increase their contribution to the labour market by changing the structure of intervention. In that respect, investment policies have proved highly relevant in some countries. Especially with regard to the latter, fiscal incentives should make it more attractive to invest in the production of goods and services rather than on financial markets.

3. Labour market and social policy

In general, the relevance of the policies of activation pursued under the European Employment Strategy (subscribed to by all four countries) for labour market improvement should to be strongly emphasized. In fact, a new contract between the unemployed and the benefit administration implies that a stricter adherence both to rights (employment or activation) and duties (acceptance of job activation offers) has already contributed to lowering unemployment.

However, the relevance and magnitude of passive policies have equally to be taken into consideration. Early exits from the labour market are a particularly sensitive field, and the advantage of placing older workers in active labour market policies instead of offering them early retirement has yet to be proved. Of course, as far as possible, older workers should be maintained in their jobs and everything should be done to enable firms and workers to do so. Training, changes in work organization and flexible working-time patterns are important policy instruments to allow this. For example, gradual retirement systems should be put in place. "Passive" early exits should no longer be financed only on the general condition of being aged, but should still be available for those with long contribution periods and those having suffered from hardship at work. The Danish "job rotation" strategy is a good example of a policy which combines human resource development with the fight against unemployment.

In general, the activation of social protection seems to be required. Not only labour market policy, but also social policy (e.g. social benefits) might lead to benefit dependence. Offering rewarding work instead is certainly one way of improving the productive contribution of social protection to economic efficiency. But this depends on the creation of institutional conditions which allow activation without pushing people out of the social safety net. This entails the provision of active (and "activation") measures and a change in incentives.

To lower unemployment and poverty traps, incentives (e.g. top-ups on benefits) should be offered. Countries have already lowered disincentives, such as high marginal tax rates, and offered incentives through in-work benefits. Other means such as tax allowances (recently introduced in Ireland) and even a negative income tax should be used to "activate" those willing to work. But two things should be avoided. First, in the absence of suitable job offers (or opportunities to participate in measures), passive benefits have to be maintained, because supply cannot simply create its own demand. Second, there should be a tightly meshed safety net for those enduring real hardship in order to prevent exclusion: this concerns, for example, those marginalized because of health impairment, and single parents in crucial phases of their own and their children's lives.

A staged classification of those out of work that measures their distance from the regular labour market (such as in the Netherlands) should be used to determine the needs of policy intervention for each individual unemployed.

4. Social protection

For other fields of social protection, such as health care, invalidity benefits and pension systems, the Dutch experience offers interesting insights and solutions. It shows that government's role in regulating social protection might not mean that the government is also the provider of social security, nor even the administrator. This can be "outsourced" to the social partners, or even to private organizations and companies. However, not all public administration has been shown to be inefficient and not all private institutions are efficient. Decisions on how to administer and implement social policies should be preceded by a thorough check of the possibilities to reform public administrations. That is to say, such decisions should be taken not on ideological, but on efficiency grounds, and efficiency should not be judged on a short-term, narrow cost-benefit analysis, but should include a long-term view and the wider societal implications. There should also be some reversibility in such decisions: when private organizations are found to be inefficient the possibility to revert to public organizations should not be excluded a priori.

Some developments accompanying reform of the Welfare State seem to indicate that the supervisory role of the government has to be enforced in order to prevent workers or the unemployed suffering from severe cutbacks. Monitoring and evaluation of such reforms are therefore essential for further progress.

5. Monitoring systems

Systems for monitoring such changes should be established. For this targets have to be established and their attainment inspected at regular intervals. Barriers to goal attainment have to be discussed and policies altered accordingly. As can be seen from the example of the European Employment Strategy, monitoring is a process which helps ensure that policies do not remain mere blueprints, but are effectively implemented.

6. Equal opportunity policies

As far as equality of opportunity policies are concerned, a clear trend emerges: more and more women will participate in the labour market, as seen by low gender differentials between the labour market behaviour of younger and better-educated age groups. More heterogeneity goes with increasing labour market participation of women. Different models of participation develop, and it is improbable that they will result in a single model. Various kinds of labour market participation do exist (such as part-time and full-time work, differently split between family members) and the best policies will be those which open up a choice for participation in accordance with family considerations, which should affect not only women, but also men. Such preferences have to be matched with labour demand. For example, childcare facilities must be increased and working-time flexibility offered. Job-rotation models in combination with parental leave might increase flexibility and ensure that a temporary withdrawal from employment does not break the link with the labour market. With regard to equality of opportunity policies, Denmark, in particular, offers a good example of a possible future for the other countries as well.

ANNEXES

SOME COMPARATIVE ASPECTS BETWEEN THE UNITED STATES AND EUROPE

Although the United States has had a somewhat higher GDP growth rate than the European Union (2.4 per cent against 2.0 per cent annual average growth of real GDP from 1985 to 1995), it is not economic growth that is the real problem in Europe, but employment and unemployment. During the same period, employment in Europe grew by only 0.4 per cent annually, while it increased by 1.5 per cent in the United States. On average the unemployment rate over this period stood at 10 per cent in Europe and 6.3 per cent in the United States, and this gap has even worsened for Europe up until very recently. However, Ireland, Austria and the Netherlands had higher GDP growth rates than the United States (an annual average of 5.0 per cent for Ireland and 2.6 per cent for both Austria and the Netherlands from 1985 to 1995); and while Ireland had the same employment growth rates over the period as the United States, they were even higher for the Netherlands but lower for Austria. Between 1996 and 1998, Denmark also experienced both higher economic growth and higher employment growth than the United States. All four countries now have unemployment rates that are lower than or comparable to the United States.

Of course, these countries are small, and it is the bigger European countries such as Germany, Italy and France – which account for around 60 per cent of European GDP, 53 per cent of its employed and 60 per cent of its unemployed – that make the European situation look less favourable.

However, there are clearly countries, irrespective of their size, which have all the elements of the European system, such as corporatist governance with collective wage bargaining, and social and employment protection, and still have a good employment record without sacrificing efficiency.

EFFICIENCY AND EQUITY

When comparing the United States with some European countries, one fact is outstanding: in the United States, higher efficiency (measured here very grossly as GDP per head) goes with much lower equity than in Europe (table I.1).

Table I.1 provides a snapshot of the situation of various European countries and the United States at the beginning/middle of the 1990s. It shows that one of the richest nations of the world is also the most unequal among developed countries, as measured by income distribution measures such as the Gini coefficient and by the percentage of people in the lowest and highest income percentiles. While in the United States there is

Table I.1. Real GDP per head, income distribution and poverty (rankings in brackets)

Country	Real GDP/head PPP ($ billion)[1]	Gini coefficient[2]	Lowest 10%[3]	Highest 10%[3]	Poverty[4]	Efficiency in poverty reduction	
						Before social transfers	After social transfers
Austria	21 322(3)	23.1(8)	4.4(1)	26.8(3)	n.a.	n.a.	n.a.
Denmark	21 983(2)	24.7(7)	3.6(3)	20.5(7)	7.5(4)	36.6(6)	5.5(7)
Ireland	17 590(8)	35.9(2)	2.5(5)	27.4(2)	11.1(3)	44.7(3)	19.6(2)
Netherlands	19 876(6)	31.5(5)	2.9(4)	24.7(5)	6.7(5)	43.6(4)	9.9(6)
Germany	20 370(5)	28.1(6)	3.7(2)	22.6(6)	5.9(6)	40.5(5)	10.3(5)
France	21 176(4)	32.7(3)	2.5(5)	24.9(4)	7.5(4)	44.9(2)	12.6(3)
United Kingdom	19 302(7)	32.6(4)	2.4(6)	24.7(5)	13.5(2)	45.1(1)	12.4(4)
United States	26 977(1)	40.1(1)	1.5(7)	28.5(1)	19.1(1)	35.8(7)	23.2(1)

PPP: purchasing power parity.
Notes: [1]1995. [2]End of 1980s/beginning of 1990s: the Gini coefficient is a measure for concentration between the values 0 = equal distribution and 1 = total concentration. [3]In percentage of population percentiles ranked by income per capita. [4]Population below 50 per cent of median disposable income, late 1980s/early 1990s. [5]Population below 50 per cent of median disposable income before and after social transfers, late 1980s/early 1990s.
Sources: UNDP: *Human Development Report, 1998*; World Bank: *World Development Report, 1998/99*; van Ginneken, 1996; Cichon, 1997.

less "spontaneous" market-driven poverty, the country ends up with by far the highest percentage of poor people among the countries shown in table I.1 because of the inadequacy of transfer payments. The latter help to reduce poverty to a large extent in the European countries. The difference between the "before" and "after" social transfer rates sheds some doubt on the efficiency in poverty reduction of the Earned Income Tax Credit (a "negative income tax" for the "working poor" which has been extended by the Clinton administration).

Among the four countries under review, only Ireland still has substantial poverty rates, even after taking transfer payments into account. According to a recent Eurostat survey of those individuals who earn less than half the average household income, Ireland is among the four European countries with the highest income poverty (along with Portugal, the United Kingdom and Greece), while Austria ranks second best (on a par with Germany) after Denmark. The Netherlands follow in third place along with Belgium. O'Connell (1999) shows that poverty has increased in Ireland recently. Unfortunately, the lack of available data makes it difficult to compare poverty over time for the four countries under review, as the definitions of poverty (40, 50 or 60 per cent of median or average individual or household gross or net or disposable income) vary over time. All the same, in all of them (the least in Ireland) "spontaneous" poverty seems to have been reduced quite substantially by social transfers, and this of course imposes a certain cost. Government expenditure on social security is clearly inversely related to the incidence of poverty (with the exception of the United Kingdom, with high social spending and high income poverty) and in 1994 was around or above 30 per cent of GDP in Denmark (34 per cent), the Netherlands (32.3 per cent) and Austria (29.4 per cent), but only 21.1 per cent in Ireland. Yet even Ireland spends significantly more of its GDP than the United States, at 16 per cent (BMAGS, 1997; Cichon, 1997).

There are many other differences between the United States and EU countries that are also pertinent here, for example working time, which is much lower in Europe than in the United States. This is due to longer weekly working hours and much shorter vacations, which are on average 12 days in the United States and – depending on the country – up to 31 days in Europe's developed Welfare States. As a result, annual working time in 1994 stood at 1,568 hours in Denmark, 1,447 in the Netherlands and 1,747 in Ireland, but was 1,947 in the United States). Bosch (1999) shows that short working hours are a "luxury good" and can usually only be afforded if GDP per hour is high and wage differentiation low. Also, health coverage is less universal in the United States than in Europe. All this adds up to different types of society, with different roles ascribed to society, the State and the individual. While the share of GDP paid as employee compensation is about 10 percentage points higher in the United States than in Europe because of employment creation, this does not in general result in a more affluent society, once redistributional aspects are brought into the picture. As Cichon (1997, p. 29) notes, the European model is based on "high productivity and relatively high wages, high unemployment and decent levels of social transfers", while the American model is based on "low(er) productivity and low(er) wages, low unemployment and low transfers".

It seems that at least in some of the smaller European States, unemployment has been brought down to low levels despite high wages and high productivity, and the maintenance of a decent level of social welfare and leisure. If this is sustainable, then we will be able to speak of a European renaissance, one which is only partly explicable in terms of traditional economic analysis, but which seems above all to be linked to a certain amount of social cohesion and solidarity in Europe's national States. Greater income disparity, which seems to go hand in hand with more poverty, also has a negative effect on society, as shown by the high crime rates and prison population in the United States.

RANKING OF COUNTRIES: WHO'S THE WINNER?

Although we refrain from an explicit overall ranking of the four countries, because of the difficulties outlined in the conclusion to Chapter 2, we provide an overview of their position in existing rankings of employment, human development performance and competitiveness.

The Bertelsmann Foundation has ranked countries since 1994. This is done at two-year intervals, based on a multicausal approach using seven weighted indicators, which, according to its authors, explain 65 per cent of the difference in international employment performance. These seven indicators are: the share of investment in GDP (weight 18 per cent); the share of public expenditure in GDP (weight −9 per cent); the share of active measures in total labour market policy outlays (weight 23 per cent); the share of long-term unemployment in total unemployment (weight −16 per cent); the increase in nominal unit labour costs (−10 per cent); strike rates (weight −16 per cent); and the share of part-time workers (weight 8 per cent).

Positive weights mean "the more the better", while negative weights mean "the less the better". The target values (i.e. the measure of employment performance) consist of both the unemployment rate and the employment growth rate.

In the 1998 ranking of 20 countries, the four countries are positioned in places 4 (Austria), 8 (the Netherlands), 12 (Denmark) and 17 (Ireland). Austria and Ireland maintained their position between 1996 and 1998, while Denmark moved up two positions and the Netherlands improved by one position (see Schröder and Suntum, 1996 and 1998; figure II.1).

We cannot offer a full critique of this approach here (which would imply developing a competing model), but even without such a model it should be clear that the inclusion of other indicators (e.g. employment/unemployment flows, a dummy for the existence or not of social dialogue, domestic demand and exports, working time, dominant type of household, etc.) would change ranks considerably. A different weighting of the indicators, a different time frame and even a change in some of the assumptions would also lead to changes in positions. For example, employment achievements in Austria are largely due to increasing or more efficiently spent public funds, as recent net employment creation has been exclusively public. It seems illogical therefore to put a negative value on government expenditure, which can lead to positive employment growth and results in a top position in the performance ranking. (For a critical discussion on other factors see European Commission, 1998b.)

Figure II.1. International employment ranking, 1996 and 1998

	1996				1998		
1	Japan	8.8		1	Japan	8.8	➡
2	Switzerland	8.2		2	Switzerland	7.8	➡
3	Portugal	7.4		3	Norway	7.7	⬆ + 2
4	Austria	7.3		4	Austria	7.5	➡
5	Norway	7.3		5	United States	7.4	⬆ + 2
6	Sweden	7.2		6	Portugal	7.1	⬇ – 3
7	United States	7.1		7	New Zealand	7.0	⬆ + 3
8	Germany	7.0		8	Netherlands	6.8	↗ + 1
9	Netherlands	6.9		9	Germany	6.5	↘ – 1
10	New Zealand	6.3		10	Sweden	6.4	⬇ – 4
11	Australia	6.0		11	Australia	6.4	➡
12	Great Britain[1]	5.8		12	Denmark	6.1	⬆ + 2
13	France	5.8		13	Canada	6.0	⬆ + 2
14	Denmark	5.8		14	Great Britain[1]	5.9	⬇ – 2
15	Canada	5.8		15	France	5.7	⬇ – 2
16	Belgium	5.7		16	Belgium	5.5	➡
17	Ireland	5.1		17	Ireland	5.4	➡
18	Italy	5.0		18	Italy	4.9	➡
19	Finland 4.7			19	Finland 3.7		➡
20	Spain 3.3			20	Spain 2.8		➡

Note: [1]Includes England, Scotland and Wales
Source: Schröder and Suntum (1996 and 1998).

Another recent ranking has been made by the European Commission in its *Joint Employment Report* (1998). Composite indicators for overall employment performance have been calculated (figure II.2). Countries are not explicitly ranked, but charts presenting the composite indicators for the 15 countries plus the United States and

Figure II.2.   Comparison of labour market situations: Overall performance, 1992 and 1997

Overall

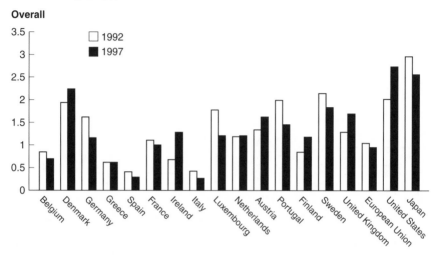

Note: This chart compares the overall labour market performances of the EU Member States, Japan and the United States, by using a composite indicator that takes simultaneously into account eight different dimensions: total employment, job growth, employment of aged people, total unemployment, youth unemployment, long-term unemployment and gender gaps in employment and unemployment. Equal weight is attached to each of these dimensions.
Source: European Commission: *Joint Employment Report*, 1998, Internet version.

Japan permit a ranking. Values are based on eight indicators of equal weight: employment rate, job growth, total unemployment, employment of older workers, youth unemployment, long-term unemployment and gender gaps in employment and unemployment. The changes between 1992 and 1997 can also be seen. By far the best performers, according to this ranking, are the United States and Japan, followed by countries such as Denmark, Sweden, the United Kingdom, Austria and Ireland. The Netherlands has a similar overall performance to Germany. While performance improved in the United States, it worsened in Japan between 1992 and 1997. The four countries under review all improved their labour market performance between 1992 and 1997, in particular Ireland and Denmark.

A composite indicator on unemployment (including total unemployment, youth unemployment, long-term unemployment and the gender gap in unemployment) shows Denmark and Austria among the best European performers, while the Netherlands ranks equal with Ireland after countries such as Sweden, the United Kingdom, Portugal and Germany (figure II.3).

This ranking shows that the weighting given to different indicators is crucial and should be based on a convincing model, rather than on the mere assumption of equal worth of each individual indicator. Indicators of structures (starting levels) and trends (development over time) should be clearly divided. (The rankings above are based on the Internet version of the *Joint Employment Report* from October 1998).

Another ranking of interest, focusing not on employment but on human development, is the human development index (HDI) produced since 1990 by the United

Figure II.3. Unemployment performance, 1992 and 1997

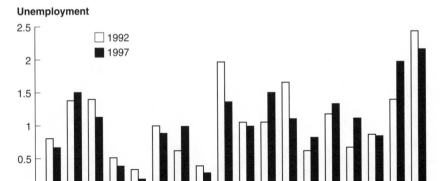

Unemployment

Note: This chart compares the unemployment performances of the EU Member States, Japan and the United States, by using a composite indicator that takes simultaneously into account four different dimensions: total employment, youth unemployment, long-term unemployment and the gender gap in unemployment. Equal weight is attached to each of these dimensions.
Source: European Commission: *Joint Employment Report*, 1998, Internet version.

Nations Development Programme (UNDP). The HDI includes three areas of human development: longevity, knowledge and standard of living. These are measured by life expectancy at birth, the adult literacy rate, and a combined enrolment rate in education and an adjusted per capita income in purchasing power parity (PPP) $. In addition, for the first time in the 1998 report, a human poverty index has been calculated for developed countries. The so-called HPI-2 index includes the percentage of people not expected to survive to age 60, the functional illiteracy rate, the percentage of people living below the poverty line (50 per cent of median disposable income) and the long-term unemployment rate. Moreover, gender-related indices have also been calculated. The GDI (gender-related development index) is the HDI index adjusted downward for gender inequality, measuring the difference between the male and female HDIs for a given country. The GEM (gender empowerment measure) measures women's active participation in economic and political life in terms of the differences in income between men and women, the percentage of women in parliament, among managers and administrators, and among professional and technical workers. The rankings are shown in table II.1.

While these rankings are difficult to compare because of different ranking intervals, they show that three out of our four countries are among the richest in the world in GDP per capita terms; only Ireland still lags somewhat behind, but is quickly catching up. While Ireland is close to countries such as Denmark and Germany in the HDI ranking, it performs less well in both gender-related ranks. Denmark is among the best performers in the GDP ranking per head, and also has a position among the top 20 in the HDI ranking, but is outperformed by the Netherlands with regard to the latter. Denmark is also a top performer in both gender dimensions, especially in

Table II.1. Rankings in different human development measures, various industrialized countries[1]

Country	GDP/head[2]	HDI[3]	HPI-2[2]	GDI[4]	GEM[5]
Austria	6	13	n.a.	15	10
Denmark	3	18	9	10	3
Ireland	15	17	16	27	21
Netherlands	10	7	2	12	9
Germany	8	19	3	17	8
France	7	2	7	7	31
United Kingdom	12	14	15	11	20
United States	1	4	17	6	11
Japan	4	8	8	13	38

Notes: [1] Figures usually refer to 1995. [2] Ranks from 1 to 17. [3] Ranks from 1 to 174. [4] Ranks from 1 to 163. [5] Ranks from 1 to 102.

Source: UNDP: *Human Development Report*, 1998.

terms of women's access to political influence (GEM). The Netherlands is well placed in all positions, and especially in the poverty index. The United States is a top performer in GDP per head and in HDI, but is last among all the industrialized countries ranked in the human poverty index. There is no space here to discuss the different indices, but the general observation that the choice of indicators and their weighing is crucial also applies to the human development ranking (see also more general remarks on ranking, below).

Other types of rankings are based more strongly on economic indicators. A prominent example is the World Competitiveness Report, established by the International Institute of Management Development (IMD) in Lausanne, Switzerland, which since 1987 has established country competitiveness rankings for 46 countries using 259 criteria (table II.2). These criteria are based two-thirds on empirical data on competitiveness and one-third on surveys of perceived competitiveness. Criteria include productivity, price stability, innovation, social stability, state intervention, qualification of the workforce, level of technology, investments and other items.

Table II.2. World competitiveness, 1994 and 1998

Country	1994	1998
Austria	11	22
Denmark	7	8
France	13	21
Germany	6	14
Ireland	21	11
Netherlands	8	4
United Kingdom	14	12
United States	1	1

Source: IMD, 1998.

According to this ranking, two of the countries under review have increased their competitiveness, while one (Denmark) has remained rather stable and another (Austria) has fallen back. Again, in order to properly judge such a ranking, an analysis of the different indicators and their respective weights, and the underlying assumptions, is required, which cannot be done in the present study. A critical remark on poor rankings is required, however: the bad ranking of Ireland in 1994 has not prevented a dramatic increase in inward investment, pushing the country up the scale. That is, investors seem not to have taken the ranking seriously.

SOME GENERAL PROBLEMS OF RANKINGS

Rankings are attractive because they give the illusion of simplicity, reducing complex interrelations to simple numbers. Complex methods and complex indicators based on data derived from sources of varying credibility make it very difficult to trace the way in which the positions were established, unless substantial time and money are committed to such checks. Therefore they are very difficult to control for accuracy. And, as it is usually impossible to have comparative statistics on each variable for each country, rankings are based often on heroic estimates. Changes in indicators (or in weights given to indicators) have a profound impact on rankings. Moreover, indicators are usually based on assumptions which are ideologically biased. In particular, ranking with compound indicators should only be used carefully, and assumptions, indicators and weights should be known. In general, such compound rankings should be considered a starting-point for a deeper analysis rather than as a result showing the objective ranking of countries.

EDUCATION AND TRAINING

For many years now, education and training have been singled out as one of the most prominent factors for economic growth besides labour and capital. Growth accounting studies (Denison, 1988) have shown that, in the United States, for example, most of the residuals of growth are explained by increases in education, once the contributions of capital, labour and land are accounted for. While these studies refer more to the level of general education (enrolment and expenditure), later studies have pointed out the importance of vocational training and training systems in general for productivity (Steedman and Wagner, 1987; Prais, 1989). The *World Employment Report 1998/99* (ILO, 1998) shows in particular the importance of lifelong education and training for the world's economic development.

While it is highly probable that education and training (ET) systems have contributed to the employment success of the four countries (e.g. it is estimated that Irish human capital investment policies have contributed 0.6 percentage points to economic growth), the magnitude of this contribution across countries is difficult to estimate because of a lack of comparative data. In their absence, we will merely describe some of the possible contributions made by ET in a more qualitative fashion.

While the figures in table III.1 are not strictly comparable, as they come from different sources (but have their origin in the European labour force surveys), they still suggest that major changes seem to be under way in national systems: if we consider the 16–29 year-olds as a quasi cohort, we see that Ireland is about to dramatically improve its education system, and now has among its younger population the lowest percentage of those with only basic education. However, it has still the highest percentage in its prime-aged workforce. In all other countries, the percentage of those having only basic education seems to have risen, most dramatically in Denmark; but this could also simply be an effect of specific training systems and adult education opportunities in Denmark, which provide skills later on, thus equalizing out the skills balance. The lower figure for the 16–29 year-olds compared with the prime-aged workforce in tertiary education could indicate that students stay longer in education than elsewhere. Austria has apparently increased its university enrolment rates, but saw both an increase in those with only basic education and a decrease in those with upper secondary education. Again, attainment levels for the young will change as more skills are acquired during working life.

Different ET systems exist in the four countries. As far as vocational training is concerned, Austria runs an apprenticeship system (the so-called "dual" system, as it implies

Table III.1. Educational attainment of the age groups 25–49 (1) and 16–29 (2), 1996 (percentage distribution)

Country	L(1)	L(2)	M(1)	M(2)	H(1)	H(2)
Austria	27.4	31.4	64.0	56.2	8.6	12.4
Denmark	21.0	51.8	50.0	36.4	29.0	11.8
Ireland	48.1	26.5	28.4	40.9	23.4	32.6
Netherlands	35.2	37.1[1]	42.0	48.5[1]	22.5	14.4[1]
EU 15	41.6	–	38.4	–	18.8	–

Notes: L: less than upper secondary; M: upper secondary; H: university/tertiary. [1]Data for 1994.
Sources: L(1)–H(1): Eurostat: *Labour Force Survey, Results 1996*; L(2)–H(2): OECD: *Employment Outlook*, 1998.

alternating between education and work) which has contributed to low entry unemployment for youth. It seems also to be an ingenious solution for cost sharing between the firms (which provide training places), individuals (who earn low entry wages) and the Government (which provides theoretical training through vocational schools). It provides the economy with a solid basis of specialized medium-level skills, but is said to be slow to adapt to new skill demands (e.g. hybrid skills). However, the system has undergone changes and the number of specialized professions has been reduced, rendering the skill profiles of the remaining professions much broader. The Government usually subsidizes apprenticeship when firms do not offer enough training places. Yet, while the system is still the most important element of vocational training, school-based, secondary-level vocational training is becoming increasingly important. The figures on educational attainment (table III.1) show that the focus is on medium-level skills, while Austria has comparatively rather low attainment rates in higher education, which might be a barrier to growth in high-technology product and service segments.

Apprenticeship systems also exist in the Netherlands and to some extent in Denmark, whereas they are rare in Ireland. In the latter, around 80 per cent of vocational training is located in schools (Rubery, forthcoming). When vocational skills are not developed in firms, but in vocational schools only, a gap between "real" working life and the schools might exist, which could reduce the capacity of vocational training to act as a bridge into employment. Such a development can, for example, be seen in France (with very high entry unemployment and a difficult education-labour market transition) and might occur also in Austria, if more emphasis were put on vocational training schools, rather than on apprenticeships (such a development is suggested by Pichelmann, with Hofer, 1999).

The Danish system is an example of a rather comprehensive organization of life-long learning through further training, which is part of labour market policy, but extends beyond. Enrolment figures for further training are highest in Denmark, and the further training system is part of the specific employment system established there. It provides for short modules of training with nationwide validity in many professions, and thus underpins labour mobility. The figures in table III.1 (showing a rather unbalanced attainment level for the younger group, but a much more equal skills balance for prime ages) might also therefore be an indication of the success of the further training system.

Table III.2. Computers (per 1,000 people) and Internet hosts
(per 10,000 people)

Country	Computers (1996)	Internet (July 1997)
Austria	148.0	108.25
Denmark	304.1	259.73
Ireland	145.0	91.0
Netherlands	232.0	219.0
Germany	233.2	106.68
United States	362.4	442.11

Source: World Bank: *World Development Report 1998/99.*

In Ireland, while in the past many people had only basic schooling and there was a lack of intermediate-level qualifications, the changes in the last 20 years have altered the skills balance tremendously. In particular, the high percentage of those with higher education shows that Ireland's education authorities are quite successful in providing skills for the higher end of the labour market, promoting growth in, for example, information technology products and services. This might help to explain why Ireland has become the world's largest software exporter outside the United States.

In Austria, Denmark and the Netherlands, the social partners are involved in the design and implementation of vocational training. There seems to be some lack of involvement of the social partners in this crucial field in Ireland, although vocational training issues are being discussed at the central level. However, social dialogue should be extended to the whole ET system and not only concern elements of it. It is highly probable that some specific structures of the whole education and training system and its interrelations (i.e. vocational and general education, as well as higher, secondary and primary education) are more adapted than others to support an employment-intensive growth path.

As the workforce ages, lifelong learning becomes an increasingly important part of any growth-oriented education and training strategy. Larsson (1999) has shown that the speed of technological innovation and that at which workforce skills are renewed are far apart: while 80 per cent of the technology used today will be outdated by 2005, 80 per cent of the workforce will then be operating on the basis of formal education and training that are at least ten years old.

It is also possible that the concentration on formal education hides some of the more informal processes of skill acquisition. On the one hand, with computer technology the gap between general and company-specific skills (Becker, 1975) becomes increasingly blurred (e.g. someone trained on Microsoft programmes can use this training in most firms). On the other hand, access to computers and the Internet could be an advantage for formal as well as for informal (home-based) training. In that context, statistics show that the penetration of these new technologies is particularly high in the United States, but also in Denmark and in the Netherlands, while both Ireland and Austria are lagging somewhat behind (see table III.2). This seems at first sight a contradiction to what was said about Ireland, but being a performing software exporter does not tell us much about the use being made of information technology in the domestic market.

COMMITMENT THREE OF THE WORLD SUMMIT ON SOCIAL DEVELOPMENT

We commit ourselves to promoting the goal of full employment as a basic priority of our economic and social policies, and to enabling all men and women to attain secure and sustainable livelihoods through freely chosen productive employment and work.

To this end, at the national level, we will:

(a) Put the creation of employment, the reduction of unemployment and the promotion of appropriately and adequately remunerated employment at the centre of strategies and policies of Governments, with full respect for workers' rights and with the participation of employers, workers and their respective organizations, giving special attention to the problems of structural, long-term unemployment and underemployment of youth, women, people with disabilities, and all other disadvantaged groups and individuals;

(b) Develop policies to expand work opportunities and productivity in both rural and urban sectors by achieving economic growth, investing in human resource development, promoting technologies that generate productive employment, and encouraging self-employment, entrepreneurship, and small and medium-sized enterprises;

(c) Improve access to land, credit, information, infrastructure and other productive resources for small and micro-enterprises, including those in the informal sector, with particular emphasis on the disadvantaged sectors of society;

(d) Develop policies to ensure that workers and employers have the education, information and training needed to adapt to changing economic conditions, technologies and labour markets;

(e) Explore innovative options for employment creation and seek new approaches to generating income and purchasing power;

(f) Foster policies that enable people to combine their paid work with their family responsibilities;

(g) Pay particular attention to women's access to employment, the protection of their position in the labour market and the promotion of equal treatment of women and men, in particular with respect to pay;

(h) Take due account of the importance of the informal sector in our employment development strategies with a view to increasing its contribution to the eradication of poverty and to social integration in developing countries, and to strengthening its linkages with the formal economy;

(i) Pursue the goal of ensuring quality jobs, and safeguard the basic rights and interests of workers and to this end, freely promote respect for relevant International Labour Organization Conventions, including those on the prohibition of forced and child labour, the freedom of association, the right to organize and bargain collectively, and the principle of non-discrimination;

(j) Ensure that migrant workers benefit from the protections provided by relevant national and international instruments, take concrete and effective measures against the exploitation of migrant workers, and encourage all countries to consider the ratification and full implementation of the relevant international instruments on migrant workers;

(k) Foster international cooperation in macroeconomic policies, liberalization of trade and investment so as to promote sustained economic growth and the creation of employment, and exchange experiences on successful policies and programmes aimed at increasing employment and reducing unemployment.

THE EMPLOYMENT POLICY CONVENTION, 1964 (NO. 122)
[operative paragraphs]

The General Conference of the International Labour Organization,

Having been convened at Geneva by the Governing Body of the International Labour Office, and having met in its Forty-eighth Session on 17 June 1964, and Considering that the Declaration of Philadelphia recognizes the solemn obligation of the International Labour Organization to further among the nations of the world programmes which will achieve full employment and the raising of standards of living, and that the Preamble to the Constitution of the International Labour Organization provides for the prevention of unemployment and the provision of an adequate living wage, and

Considering further that under the terms of the Declaration of Philadelphia it is the responsibility of the International Labour Organization to examine and consider the bearing of economic and financial policies upon employment policy in the light of the fundamental objective that all human beings, irrespective of race, creed or sex, have the right to pursue both their material well-being and their spiritual development in conditions of freedom and dignity, of economic security and equal opportunity, and

Considering that the Universal Declaration of Human Rights provides that everyone has the right to work, to free choice of employment, to just and favourable conditions of work and to protection against unemployment, and

Noting the terms of existing international labour Conventions and Recommendations of direct relevance to employment policy, and in particular of the Employment Service Convention and Recommendation, 1948, the Vocational Guidance Recommendation, 1949, the Vocational Training Recommendation, 1962, and the Discrimination (Employment and Occupation) Convention and Recommendation, 1958, and

Considering that these instruments should be placed in the wider framework of an international programme for economic expansion on the basis of full, productive and freely chosen employment, and

Having decided upon the adoption of certain proposals with regard to employment policy, which are included in the eighth item on the agenda of the session, and

Having determined that these proposals shall take the form of an international Convention,

adopts the ninth day of July of the year one thousand nine hundred and sixty-four, the following Convention, which may be cited as the Employment Policy Convention, 1964:

Article 1

1. With a view to stimulating economic growth and development, raising levels of living, meeting manpower requirements and overcoming unemployment and underemployment, each Member shall declare and pursue, as a major goal, an active policy designed to promote full, productive and freely chosen employment.

2. The said policy shall aim at ensuring that:

(a) there is work for all who are available for and seeking work;
(b) such work is as productive as possible;
(c) there is freedom of choice of employment and the fullest possible opportunity for each worker to qualify for, and to use his skills and endowments in, a job for which he is well suited, irrespective of race, colour, sex, religion, political opinion, national extraction or social origin.

3. The said policy shall take due account of the stage and level of economic development and the mutual relationships between employment objectives and other economic and social objectives, and shall be pursued by methods that are appropriate to national conditions and practices.

Article 2

Each Member shall, by such methods and to such extent as may be appropriate under national conditions:

(a) decide on and keep under review, within the framework of a coordinated economic and social policy, the measures to be adopted for attaining the objectives specified in Article 1;
(b) take such steps as may be needed, including when appropriate the establishment of programmes, for the application of these measures.

Article 3

In the application of this Convention, representatives of the persons affected by the measures to be taken, and in particular representatives of employers and workers, shall be consulted concerning employment policies, with a view to taking fully into account their experience and views and securing their full cooperation in formulating and enlisting support for such policies.

Articles 4–11: standard final provisions.

BIBLIOGRAPHY

Alan, Ch.S. 1997. "Institutions challenged: German unification, policy errors and the 'siren song of deregulation'", in L. Turner: *Negotiating the new Germany: Can social partnership survive?* (Ithaca, New York, Cornell University Press).

Albert, M. 1993. *Capitalisme contre capitalisme* (Paris, Editions du Seuil).

Auer, P. 1994. "Further education and training for the employed: Systems and outcomes", in G. Schmid (ed.): *Labour market institutions in Europe* (New York, M.E. Sharpe).

——. 1998. "Participation and employment rates: Convergence or divergence?", in P. Auer (ed.): *Employment policies in focus* (Berlin, European Commission).

—— (ed.). Forthcoming. *Labour market institutions for decent work* (Geneva, ILO).

——; Kruppe, T. 1996. "Monitoring of labour market policy in EU member states", in G. Schmid et al.: *International handbook of labour market policy and evaluation* (Cheltenham, Edward Elgar), pp. 899–923.

Axelrod, R. 1984. *The evolution of cooperation* (New York, Basic Books).

Becker, G.S. 1975. *Human capital* (New York, National Bureau for Economic Research).

Bosch, G. Forthcoming. "Working-time policies", in Auer (ed.), forthcoming.

Bundesministerium für Arbeit, Gesundheit und Soziales (BMAGS). 1997. *Bericht über die soziale Lage 1996* (Vienna).

Bureau voor Economische Argumentatie (KPMG). 1998. *The public employment service in the Netherlands*, research report (Hoofdorp).

Buti, M.; Pench, L.R.; Sestito, P. 1998. *European unemployment: Contending theories and institutional complexities*, document 11/81/98, European Commission, DGII and Forward Studies Unit (Brussels).

Calmfors, L.; Driffill, J. 1988. "Bargaining structure, corporatism and macroeconomic performance", in *Economic Policy*, Apr., pp. 15–61.

Cazes, S.; Boeri, T.; Bertola, G. 1999. *Employment protection and labour market adjustment in OECD countries: Evolving institutions and variable enforcement*, Employment and Training Paper, No. 48 (Geneva, ILO).

Cichon, M. 1997. *Are there better ways to cut and share the cake?*, Issues in Social Protection, Discussion Paper 3 (Geneva, ILO, Social Security Department).

Crouch, C. 1993. *Industrial relations and European state traditions* (Oxford, Clarendon).

Denison, E. 1988. *Accounting for United States economic growth* (Washington, DC, The Brookings Institution).

Dercksen, H.J.; de Koning, J. 1996. *The new public employment service in the Netherlands*, Discussion Paper FSI 96-201 (Berlin, Wissenschaftszentrum).

Döhrn, R.; Heilmann, U.; Schäfer G. 1998. "Ein dänisches Beschäftigungswunder?", in *Mitteilungen aus der Arbeitsmarkt und Berufsforschung*, 2/1998.

European Commission. 1993. *Growth, competitiveness and employment*, White Paper (Luxembourg).

——. 1996. *Labour market studies (*four reports: *Denmark, Ireland, Austria, Netherlands* (Brussels).

——. 1997. *Modernising and improving social protection in the European Union*, Communication from the Commission, COM(97) 1021 (Luxembourg).

——. 1998a. *Adapting and promoting the social dialogue at Community level*, Commission Communication of 20 May 1998.

——. 1998b. *Benchmarking employment performance and labour market policies*, Employment Observatory Research Network (Berlin, Institute for Applied Socioeconomics).

——. 1998c. *Employment Observatory Trends* (Brussels/Berlin), No. 30, Summer.

——. 1998d. *Employment in Europe 1998* (Brussels).

——. 1998e. *Employment Rates Report* (Brussels).

——. 1998f; 1999. *Joint Employment Report* (Brussels).

European Employment Observatory (EEO) at: http://www.ias.berlin.de.

European Industrial Relations Observatory (EIRO), news and features on different issues at: http://www.eiro.eurofound.ie.

European Observatory for SMEs. 1997. *Fifth Annual Report* (Zoetermeer, Small Business Research and Consultancy).

Eurostat. 1997. *Labour Force Survey, Results 1996* (Luxembourg).

Friedmann, M. 1968. "The role of monetary policy", in *American Economic Review,* Vol. LVIII, pp. 1–17.

Frühstück, E., et al. 1998. *Die Rückkehr in ein vorübergehend aufgelöstes Beschäftigungsverhältnis* (Vienna, Synthesis).

Fynes, B., et al. 1998. "The changing nature of working time arrangements in Ireland", in *Flexible working lives,* Irish Studies in Management (Dublin, Oak Tree Press in association with the Graduate School of Business, University of Dublin).

Gazier, B. 1998. *Full employment, employment regimes and transitional labour markets: A comparative approach,* paper prepared for the Conference on Transitional Labour Markets, Wissenschaftszentrum, Berlin, Jan.

Graafland, J. 1996. "Unemployment benefits and employment: A review of empirical evidence", in van Ginneken (ed), 1996.

Gregg, P.; Wadsworth, J. 1998. "Unemployment households: Causes and consequences of employment polarisation among European countries", in *Employment Observatory Policies* (Brussels, European Commission), No. 63, Aug.

Gual, J. 1998. *Job creation: The role of labour market institutions* (Cheltenham, Edward Elgar).

Hartog, J. 1999. *So what's so special about the Dutch model?,* Employment and Training Paper No. 54 (Geneva, ILO).

Hermerijck, A.; Visser, J. 1997. *'A Dutch miracle', job growth, welfare reform and corporatism in the Netherlands* (Amsterdam, Amsterdam University Press).

Hirschmann, A.O. 1970. *Exit, voice and loyalty: Responses to decline in firms, organizations and states* (Cambridge, Massachusetts, Harvard University Press).

Hyman, R.; Ferner. A. (eds.). 1999. *New frontiers in European industrial relations* (Oxford, Blackwell).

International Labour Office (ILO). 1997. *World Employment Report 1996/97: National policies in a global context* (Geneva).

——. 1998. *World Employment Report 1998/99: Employability in the global economy – How training matters* (Geneva).

——. 1999. *Decent work,* Report of the Director-General to the 87th Session of the International Labour Conference (Geneva).

International Monetary Fund (IMF). 1998. Press information notice, No. 98/42 and 98/42 (on country reviews in Austria and the Netherlands).

Katzenstein, P.J. 1985. *Small states in world markets: Industrial policy in Europe* (Ithaca, New York, Cornell University Press).

Larsson, A. 1999. *Towards a European pact for employment,* paper presented at the ILO Transition Workshop, The Hague.

Latullipe, D. 1996. *Effective retirement age and duration of retirement in the industrial countries between 1950 and 1990,* Issues in Social Protection, Discussion Paper 2 (Geneva, ILO, Social Security Department).

Lucas, R.E. Jr. 1977. "Economic policy evaluation: A critique", in K. Brunner and A. Meltzer: *The Philips curve and labour markets* (Amsterdam, North-Holland), pp. 19–46.

Madsen, P.K. 1999. *Denmark: Labour market recovery through labour market policy,* Employment and Training Paper No. 53 (Geneva, ILO).

Meager, N. (with Evans, C.). 1998. *The evaluation of active labour market measures for the long-term unemployed,* Employment and Training Paper No. 16 (Geneva, ILO).

Meerendonk, A. 1998. *Benchmarking the German and Dutch welfare states*, Werkdokumenten No. 77 (The Hague, Ministry of Social Affairs and Employment).

Ministry of Social Affairs and Employment of the Netherlands. 1996. *The Dutch welfare state from an international and economic perspective* (The Hague).

Mutual Information System on Social Security (MISSOC), European Commission. 1996. *Soziale Sicherheit in den Mitgliedstaaten der Europäischen Union* (Luxembourg).

Netherlands Economic Institute (NEI). 1999. *Inactivity-activity rates: A descriptive analysis for selected countries* (The Hague).

O'Connell, P. 1999. *Ireland: Astonishing success – Economic growth and the labour market in Ireland,* Employment and Training Paper No. 44 (Geneva, ILO).

——; McGinnity, F. 1997. *Working schemes? Active labour market policy in Ireland* (Aldershot, Ashgate Press).

Organisation for Economic Co-operation and Development (OECD). 1995a. "Implementing the strategy", *Jobs Study* (Paris).

——. 1995b. "Taxation, employment and unemployment", *Jobs Study* (Paris).

——. 1996. "Enhancing the effectiveness of active labour market policies", *Jobs Strategy* (Paris).

——. 1997a. "Income distribution and poverty in selected OECD countries", in *Economic Outlook* (Paris), No. 62, Dec.

——. 1997b. *Employment Outlook* (Paris).

——. 1997c. *Economic Surveys* (two reports: *Ireland and Denmark*) (Paris).

——. 1998a. *Economic Surveys* (two reports: *Austria and The Netherlands*) (Paris).

——. 1998b. *Employment Outlook* (Paris).

Pichelmann, K. (with Hofer, H.). 1999. *Austria: Long-term success through social partnership,* Employment and Training Paper No. 52 (Geneva, ILO).

Prais, S.J. 1995. *Productivity, education and training: An international perspective* (Cambridge, Cambridge University Press).

Rubery, J. Forthcoming. "Equal opportunity and employment policy", in Auer (ed.), forthcoming.

Schettkat, R. Forthcoming. "Macroeconomic policy", in Auer (ed.), forthcoming.

Schmid, G. 1994. *Labour market institutions in Europe* (New York, M.E. Sharpe).

——. 1995. "Is full employment still possible? Transitional labour markets as a new strategy of labour market policy", in *Economic and Industrial Policy,* No.11, pp. 429–456.

——. 1998. *Transitional labour markets: A new European employment strategy,* discussion paper FSI 98-206 (Berlin, Wissenschaftszentrum).

Schmitter, P.C.; Lehmbruch, G. (eds.). 1979. *Trends towards corporatist intermediation* (Beverly Hills, Sage).

Schömann, K.; Kruppe, T.; Rogowski, R. 1998. "Fixed-term contracts in the European Union", in Auer, 1998, pp. 137–157.

Schröder, J.; Suntum, U. 1996 and 1998. *International Employment Ranking*, 1996 and 1998 (Gütersloh, Bertelsmann Foundation Publishers).

Steedman, H.; Wagner, K. 1987. "A second look at productivity, machinery and skills in Britain and Germany", in *National Institute Economic Review*, Nov.

Streeck, W.; Schmitter, P.C. 1985. "Community, market, state – and associations?", in W. Streeck and P.C. Schmitter (eds.): *Private interest government: Beyond market and state* (London, Sage), pp.1-29.

Traxler, F. 1999. "Austria: Still the country of corporatism", in Hyman and Ferner (eds.), 1999, pp. 239-261.

——; Kittel, B.; Lengauer, S. 1996. *Globalisation, collective bargaining and performance*, paper presented at the Eighth Conference of Socio-Economics, Geneva, 12–14 July.

Turner, L. 1998. *Negotiating the new Germany: Can social partnership survive?* (Ithaca, New York, Cornell University Press).

United Nations Development Programme (UNDP). 1997 and 1998. *Human Development Report*, 1997 and 1998 (Oxford, Oxford University Press).

Van Ginneken, W. (ed.). 1996. *Finding the balance: Financing and coverage of social protection in Europe* (Geneva, International Social Security Association), July.

Visser, J. Forthcoming. "Industrial relations and social dialogue", in Auer (ed.), forthcoming.

Waarden, F.V. 1995. "Government intervention in industrial relations", in J.V. Ruysseveldt, R. Huiskoemp and J. Van Hoof (eds.): *Comparative industrial and employment relations* (London, Sage).

Walter, S. 1998. *Taxation and the labour market* (Geneva, ILO; mimeo.).

Werner, H. 1998. "Beschäftigungspolitisch erfolgreiche Länder: Was steckt dahinter?", in *Mitteilungen aus der Arbeitmarkt- und Berufsforschung*, Vol. 2.

Wilthagen, T. 1998. *Flexicurity: A new paradigm for labour market reform?*, Discussion Paper FSI 98-202 (Berlin, Wissenschaftszentrum).

World Bank. 1999. *World Development Report 1998/99: Knowledge for development* (Washington, DC, Oxford University Press).

INDEX

Note: Tables and figures are indicated by *italic* page numbers, major treatments of subjects by **bold** numbers. Footnotes are denoted by, e.g., 34*n1*. Ranges of page numbers do not necessarily indicate continuous treatment.

active labour market policy *see* labour market policy
age groups
  employment rates 8–9, *8–9, 74*
  inactivity rates 27–9, *28*
  unemployment 24–5, 76, 84
  see also older workers; youth
ageing of workforce *see* older workers
agriculture, employment shift from 99
America *see* United States of America
Anglo-Saxon pluralist model (industrial relations) 55–7, *55*
apprenticeship 8, *90*, 93, 96, 118–19
  see also youth education/training
Asian Tiger socio-economic model 97
Australia *73, 113*
Austria *see* individual subjects

back-to-work allowance 47
Belgium 29, *30–31*, 50, *55, 58, 73*, 110, *113–15*
benefits *see* social benefits
Bertelsmann Foundation 112
Britain *see* United Kingdom
budgets, public 36, 42–3, *43*, 51, 62–3
  deficits 42, 91, 98
Bundesbank 36, 42

Canada *73, 113*
capital formation 44, *45–6*
Celtic Tiger socio-economic model 97
Central European Social Partnership (Rhineland socio-economic model) 55, *55*, 57, 97

CEPRs *see* country employment policy reviews
child labour 122
childcare 94, 106
  see also family responsibilities
collective bargaining 35–6, 52–4, 56–7, **63–6**, 89, 95, 97–8, 122
  coordination **54**, *55*, 56–7
  coverage rates 56–7, *58*
  decentralization 57–8
  wages 1, 35, 40, 53–4, *55*, 64–5, 101
Commitment Three of the World Summit for Social Development (1995) v, **121–2**
company size, employment by 13, **14**, *15*
compensation of employees *49, 60–61*, 111
competitiveness 37, 51–3
  rankings 112, 116–17, *116*
computer technology 37, 98, 120, *120*
corporate tax 46–7, 52, 92
corporatism 52–3, 56, 58, 66, **95–7**
  Northern corporatism 54–5, *55*, 57
corporatist governance 42, 54, 58, 62, **65–7**, 89–90, *90*, **95–6**
  defined 35–6
  problems **64–5**, 96, 98
  see also government; social dialogue; social partners
country employment policy reviews (CEPRs) v, **xi–xii**, 9, *13*, 71, *78, 95*
currency policy *see* monetary policy

Danube socio-economic model 97
decent work 32, 99, 101